ANOTHER SERVING

The *Kentucky Monthly* 10th Anniversary Cookbook

10-digit International Standard Book Number 0-913383-99-6
13-digit International Standard Book Number 978-0-913383-99-5
Library of Congress Card Catalog Number 2007942439

Cover design and book layout by Kelli Schreiber of *Kentucky Monthly*
Photography by Wales Hunter
Food preparation and styling by Sullivan University chefs and students

Manufactured in the United State of America

All book order correspondence should be addressed to:

McClanahan Publishing House, Inc.
P.O. Box 100
Kuttawa, KY 42055

1-800-544-6959
(270) 388-9388
(270) 388-6186 FAX

www.kybooks.com

Contents

Appetizers
&
Breads

Bourbon & Bacon Scallops

24 SERVINGS

2 cloves garlic, minced
2 tablespoons Kentucky bourbon
2 tablespoons maple syrup
1 tablespoon soy sauce
1 tablespoon Dijon mustard
1/4 teaspoon pepper
24 large sea scallops
6 bacon slices
1 large onion, quartered
1 large bell pepper, sliced

Mix garlic, bourbon, syrup, soy sauce, mustard and pepper together in a large bowl. Add scallops and stir to cover with sauce. Cover bowl and refrigerate for 1 hour.

Remove scallops, reserving liquid. Cut each bacon slice into 4 pieces and wrap each scallop. Thread scallops and bacon onto 4 skewers, alternating with sections of onion and pieces of green pepper. Place skewers onto hot grill coated with cooking spray. Baste with marinade and cook until scallops are done. Remove meat and vegetables from skewers to platter and serve with individual toothpicks.

Spinach & Artichoke Dip

12 SERVINGS

Two 10-ounce boxes frozen spinach, thawed
1/4 cup butter
2 tablespoons onion, minced
2 cloves fresh garlic, pressed
1/4 cup flour
1 pint heavy cream
1/4 cup chicken stock
2 teaspoons lemon juice
1/2 teaspoon hot sauce
1/2 teaspoon salt
2/3 cup Pecorino Romano cheese, grated
1/3 cup sour cream
12 ounce jar artichoke hearts, drained and chopped
1/2 cup white Cheddar cheese, shredded

Drain spinach well. Combine butter, onion, and garlic in a medium saucepan and sauté. Add flour; stir and cook over medium heat. Slowly add cream and stock and whisk until well-blended, then cook until boiling. Quickly add lemon juice, hot sauce, salt and Romano cheese.

Remove from heat and allow the mixture to cool. Stir in the sour cream. Add spinach and artichoke hearts. Pour into a microwave-proof bowl, top with Cheddar cheese and microwave until the cheese melts.

Serve with tortilla chips for dipping, French bread or your favorite crackers.

Buffalo Chicken Dip

12-18 SERVINGS

5 chicken breasts
12-ounce bottle Texas Pete® hot sauce
Two 8- ounce packages cream cheese
16- ounce bottle ranch dressing
1 1/2 cups celery, chopped
2 cups Monterey Jack cheese

Boil and shred the chicken, cover with the hot sauce and set aside. Melt the cream cheese in the microwave and add the ranch dressing, celery and cheese. Add chicken and mix well.

Pour into a 9x13-inch baking dish. Bake, uncovered, for 45 minutes at 350 degrees.

Serve with Frito® scoop chips.

Dockside Crab Dip

MAKES APPROXIMATELY 1 CUP

8 ounces cream cheese, softened
1/2 cup mayonnaise
1/4 cup mild Cheddar cheese, finely-grated
1 clove garlic, pressed
1 teaspoon Worcestershire sauce
Salt and pepper to taste
1 cup fresh crabmeat, shredded

Combine the cream cheese and mayonnaise and mix well. Stir in the remaining ingredients. Chill until ready to serve.

Buffalo Chicken Dip

Pineapple Cheese Ball

12-18 SERVINGS

16 ounces cream cheese, at room temperature
8-ounce can crushed pineapple, drained
1/2 green pepper, chopped
2 tablespoons onion, chopped
1 teaspoon salt
1 cup crushed pecans

Combine the cream cheese and pineapple and mix well. Add the green pepper, onion and salt; mix well. Cover and chill. Remove from the refrigerator and shape into large ball. Roll the ball in the crushed pecans and chill.

Serve with crackers.

Cheesy Bacon Ball

12 SERVINGS

8 ounces shredded sharp Cheddar cheese, at room temperature
8 ounces mayonnaise
1 bunch green onions, chopped
1 pound crispy fried bacon, drained and crumbled
Parsley for garnish (optional)

Combine the cheese and mayonnaise in a large bowl. Add the onions and bacon and mix well. Cover and chill.

Remove the cheese mixture from the refrigerator and form into 1 large ball or 2 small balls. Garnish with the parsley or roll in chopped parsley before serving.

Salmon Mousse

10 SERVINGS

10 3/4-ounce can tomato soup
10 3/4-ounce can cream of shrimp soup
8 ounces cream cheese
1 cup mayonnaise
3 tablespoons unflavored gelatin
3/4 cup water
1 cup pink or red salmon
1 1/4 cups celery, finely chopped
2 tablespoons onion, chopped
Parsley, cherry tomatoes and baby shrimp for garnish (optional)

Heat the soups, cream cheese and mayonnaise in a saucepan until mixture is bubbly. Soften the unflavored gelatin with 3/4 cup of water. Add the gelatin mixture to the soup mixture, stirring well. Cover and chill until thickened.

Remove from the refrigerator and stir in salmon, celery and onion. Mix well, then turn into a greased mold. Chill until set.

Garnish with parsley, cherry tomatoes and baby shrimp.

Celery with Beer Cheese Spread

16 SERVINGS

2 cups Cheddar cheese, shredded
3 ounces cream cheese, softened
2 tablespoons fresh parsley, minced
1 clove garlic, crushed
1/8 teaspoon salt
1/4 teaspoon hot pepper sauce
1/3 cup beer
Fresh celery, trimmed and cut into 3-inch lengths
1/2 red bell pepper, thinly sliced for garnish (optional)

Mix cheese, cream cheese, parsley, garlic, salt, pepper sauce and beer in a medium-size mixing bowl. Cover and chill for several hours.

Pipe beer cheese mixture into celery grooves using a cake decorating tool, a plastic squirt catsup bottle, or spread mixture with a knife.

Decorate with thin slices of red bell pepper.

Celery with Beer Cheese Spread

Guacamole Grande

8 SERVINGS

2 avocados, mashed
1/2 pint sour cream
1 tablespoon picante sauce, medium or hot
1 1/2 cups Monterey Jack cheese, shredded
1/2 cup green onions, chopped

Layer mashed avocados, sour cream mixed with picante sauce, cheese and green onions in a serving dish.

Serve with tortilla chips.

Stuffed Mushrooms

MAKES 24

24 large mushrooms
2 cloves garlic, minced
1 stick butter
1 cup bread crumbs
1/2 cup Parmesan cheese, grated
1/2 teaspoon salt
1/4 teaspoon pepper
2 tablespoons parsley

Remove the mushroom stems. Chop the stems finely and sauté in a skillet with the garlic and 4 tablespoons of butter. Add the bread crumbs, Parmesan cheese, salt, pepper and parsley. Pack the mushroom caps with the stuffing and place on a baking sheet. Melt the remaining butter and pour over the mushrooms. Bake at 370 degrees for 15 minutes. Serve in a chafing dish to keep warm.

Baby Hot Browns

24 SERVINGS

- 24 slices party rye bread
- 3 tablespoons butter or margarine, melted
- 3 tablespoons flour
- 1 cup milk
- 1 1/2 cups Cheddar cheese, shredded
- 1 1/2 cups turkey, cooked and diced
- 1/4 teaspoon salt
- 1/4 teaspoon ground red pepper
- 1/2 cup Parmesan cheese, grated
- 6 slices bacon, cooked and crumbled
- 5 plum tomatoes, sliced

Arrange the bread slices on a lightly coated baking sheet. Broil 6 inches from heat for 3 to 4 minutes. Set aside.

Melt the butter and add the flour. Cook 1 to 2 minutes or until smooth. Gradually whisk in the milk. Cook 1 to 2 minutes or until thick. Add the Cheddar cheese. Stir in the turkey, salt and red pepper. Top bread evenly with the mixture. Sprinkle with Parmesan cheese and half the bacon.

Bake at 500 degrees for 2 minutes or until Parmesan cheese is melted. Top with tomato slices and remaining bacon and serve.

Onion Rolls

MAKES 6

1 cup onions, finely chopped
2 tablespoons butter
Basil or dill weed
Crescent rolls or yeast rolls, refrigerated

Sauté onions in butter until tender. Season to taste with dill weed or basil. Unroll crescent or yeast rolls and spread with the mixture. Roll the dough and bake according to package directions.

Parsley & Garlic Cheese Biscuits

MAKES 12-15

2 cups biscuit mix
2/3 cup buttermilk
1/2 cup Cheddar cheese, grated
1/2 teaspoon parsley
Pinch of baking soda
Garlic powder
1 stick butter, melted

Mix first 6 ingredients together with a fork. Drop dough onto lightly-greased cookie sheet. Spoon melted butter over biscuits and bake at 450 degrees for 8 to 10 minutes.

Onion Rolls

Brown Sugar Cream Cheese Muffins

MAKES 12

1/2 cup light brown sugar, firmly packed
1/3 cup margarine, softened
3-ounces of cream cheese, softened
2/3 cup milk
1 large egg
1 teaspoon maple or vanilla extract
1 cup old-fashioned oats, uncooked
1/2 cup all-purpose flour
1/3 cup whole wheat flour
1 tablespoon baking powder
1/2 teaspoon salt
1 cup chopped pecans, divided

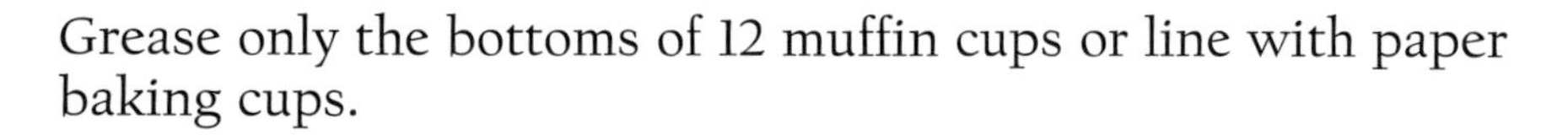

Grease only the bottoms of 12 muffin cups or line with paper baking cups.

In a medium bowl, beat the brown sugar, margarine and cream cheese with a mixer until light and fluffy. Add the milk, egg and extract, mixing well.

In another bowl, combine the oats, both flours, baking powder and salt; whisk to combine. Add 1/2 cup pecans. Combined with the sugar-butter mixture, stirring just until the dry ingredients are moistened.

Spoon the batter into the muffin cups, filling each three-quarters full. Sprinkle the remaining pecans on the tops. Bake at 400 degrees for 18 to 22 minutes, or until the muffins are golden brown.

Crème Brûlée French Toast

6 SERVINGS

1/2 cup unsalted butter
1 cup brown sugar, packed
2 teaspoons corn syrup
6 slices French bread, 1 inch thick
5 eggs
1 1/2 cups half-and-half
1 teaspoon vanilla extract
2 teaspoons orange brandy
1/4 teaspoon salt

Melt the butter in a small saucepan over medium heat. Add brown sugar and corn syrup, stirring until the brown sugar is dissolved. Pour into a 9 x 13-inch baking dish or individual crème brûlée dishes.

Arrange the bread slices in a single layer in the baking dish. Whisk the eggs, half-and-half, vanilla extract, orange brandy and salt in a small bowl. Pour over bread and cover. Chill for at least 8 hours.

Preheat the oven to 350 degrees. Remove dish from the refrigerator and allow to come to room temperature. Bake for about 35 minutes or until golden brown.

See picture on page 105.

South of the Border Corn Bread

8 SERVINGS

1 cup yellow cornmeal
1/2 teaspoon salt
2 eggs
1 cup milk
1 cup onion, chopped
1 small hot pepper, chopped
1/2 cup all-purpose flour
1/2 teaspoon baking soda
1/2 cup vegetable oil
1 cup cream-style corn
1/2 cup sharp Cheddar cheese, shredded

Combine the cornmeal, salt, eggs and milk in a large mixing bowl and mix well. Add the onion and pepper and stir. Add the flour, baking soda, oil and corn and mix well. Stir in the cheese and pour the mixture into a greased 2 quart baking dish.

Bake at 350 degrees until the top is brown.

South of the Border Corn Bread

Munchie Pretzels

10-20 SERVINGS

13.5-ounce box Snyder's® Hanover Homestyle pretzels
1 stick margarine
1 cup vegetable or canola oil
1 envelope onion soup mix

Break pretzels into bite-size pieces. Melt the margarine; add oil and onion soup mix and stir well. Add pretzel pieces and stir until all pieces are well coated.

Spread the pretzels evenly onto a cookie sheet and bake in a 250-degree oven for 1 1/2 hours or until the soup mixture has been absorbed. Let the pretzels cool. Store in an airtight container.

Cranberry Banana Walnut Bread

MAKES 1 LOAF

4 bananas, mashed
2/3 cup brown sugar
2 eggs
2 cups Bisquick®
1/4 teaspoon baking soda
1/3 cup chopped walnuts
1/2 cup dried cran-raisins

Peel and mash bananas in a large bowl. Cream sugar and eggs together in another bowl until well blended. Add bananas to the sugar mixture and stir. Pour in Bisquick® and blend. Add baking soda, walnuts and cran-raisins and stir. Pour mixture into a greased loaf pan. Bake at 350 degrees for 1 hour. Cool completely and wrap in foil.

See picture on page 105.

Derby Day Biscuits with Country Ham Filling

MAKES 12 LARGE OR 36 BITE-SIZE BISCUITS
MAKES FILLING FOR 36 BISCUITS

BISCUITS:
2 cups self-rising flour
2/3 cup shortening
2/3 cup half-and-half
COUNTRY HAM FILLING:
1 cup Kentucky country ham, cooked and ground
4 tablespoons butter, softened

Combine the flour and shortening in a large mixing bowl. Hand-mix with a pastry blender until the mixture resembles little peas. Add half-and-half and stir lightly.

Turn the mixture onto a floured surface and shape into a ball. Roll out to 1/2-inch thickness, then cut with a biscuit cutter and place biscuits on an ungreased pan. Bake in a pre-heated 450-degree oven for 10 to 12 minutes.

To prepare filling, combine the ham and butter in a small bowl. Split hot bite-size biscuits in half. Use about 1 tablespoon filling for each biscuit.

Sweet Potato Dinner Rolls

MAKES 3 DOZEN

1 medium sweet potato
2 cups water
1 envelope active dry yeast
1/3 cup sugar
1 tablespoon salt
1/2 cup butter, softened
2 eggs, beaten
5 to 6 cups all-purpose flour
Melted butter for topping (optional)

Peel and slice sweet potato. Place the potato in a saucepan with water. Cook until tender; drain, reserving 1 1/2 cups of the water. Cool the water until warm. Dissolve the yeast in the reserved water and stir.

Mash the cooked potato slices in a large bowl. Add the sugar and salt and stir in the yeast mixture. Add the butter, eggs and stir. Add 4 cups of flour, 1 cup at a time, until the mixture becomes thick. Place the mixture on a floured countertop. Add the remaining flour, a little at a time, kneading continually.

Place dough in a large, well-greased mixing bowl and turn once to coat the top. Cover with a clean cloth and let rise in a warm room until doubled, about 2 hours. Punch dough down, turn once again to grease top. Cover and refrigerate up to four days.

If you are not refrigerating for up to four days, pinch off part of the dough and roll it out on a floured counteretop. Cut into circles or triangles to make Parker House, pan or crescent rolls. Place rolls on a greased pan and let rise for an hour. Bake at 400 degrees for 15 minutes or until brown on top.

Brush with melted butter while hot.

Sweet Potato Dinner Rolls

Sorghum Wheat Rolls

MAKES 12

4 cups Weisenberger Mills® whole wheat flour
2 envelopes dry yeast
1 1/2 cups lukewarm water
1/2 cup sorghum
2 tablespoons flaxseed oil or other vegetable oil
1 tablespoon kosher salt
2 cups all-purpose flour
2 tablespoon olive oil

Combine the whole wheat flour, yeast, lukewarm water, sorghum, oil and kosher salt to make a sticky batter. Add the all-purpose flour and turn out onto a well-floured surface and knead to make an elastic dough.

Place the dough in a large bowl greased with olive oil. Cover with a damp towel and set in a warm place to rise for an hour.

After the dough has risen, punch it down and turn it out onto the floured surface again. Divide the dough into 12 portions and shape each one into a ball. Place on baking sheets lined with parchment paper. Let rise for another half-hour.

Bake at 400 degrees for 15 to 20 minutes in a preheated oven, or until golden brown. After the rolls have been removed from the oven, cool on a wire rack and enjoy them warm or at room temperature.

Soups & Salads

Beer Chili

6 SERVINGS

1 1/2 pounds ground beef
2 stalks celery, chopped
1 onion, chopped
1 green pepper, chopped
1 garlic clove, minced
6 slices bacon, cooked and crumbled
10-ounce can tomato soup
12-ounce can beer
10 ounces tomato sauce
Two 15-ounce cans kidney beans
3 tablespoons chili powder
1 1/2 teaspoons salt
1/2 teaspoon cumin
1/4 teaspoon ground cloves
2 teaspoons Accent®
1 teaspoon Mrs. Dash®
1 teaspoon hot sauce

Brown the beef and drain. Add the celery, onion and pepper and sauté, adding the garlic at the last minute. Add the remaining ingredients and mix well.

Simmer for 2 hours, adding more beer if the consistency is too thick.

Beer Chili

Low-Fat Soup

4-6 SERVINGS

Two boneless chicken breasts
Water to cover chicken
1-pound package frozen okra (not breaded)
26-ounce jar salsa
Salt and pepper
Worcestershire sauce

Place chicken, water, okra, salsa, Worcestershire sauce and seasonings in a crock pot and cook on low all day. Before serving, pull chicken apart in the broth.

Fat-Burning Cabbage Soup

12 SERVINGS

6 to 8 large green onions
One to two 28-ounce cans of tomatoes
1 large head of cabbage
2 green peppers
1 bunch of celery
1 package dry onion soup mix

Slice vegetables in small to medium pieces and completely cover with water. Add dry onion soup mix. Boil fast for 10 minutes; lower to a simmer and continue cooking until vegetables are tender.

Season with salt, pepper, curry, parsley, bouillon or hot sauce if desired.

Cream of Vegetable Soup

8 SERVINGS

2 tablespoons margarine
1 clove garlic, chopped
1 medium onion, sliced
1/4 head of cauliflower, broken
2 carrots, peeled and chopped
2 stalks celery, chopped
6 asparagus stalks, chopped
1 leek, chopped
1 large potato, peeled and chopped
1 cup spinach, chopped
Salt and pepper to taste
1 quart chicken stock
Pinch of cayenne pepper
1 cup heavy cream
3 tablespoons flour
1 tablespoon parsley, chopped
1 tablespoon Parmesan cheese

Heat margarine in a soup pot; add onion and garlic and sauté for 3 minutes.

Add vegetables, seasoning and cook 5 to 6 minutes. Pour in chicken stock; simmer 25 minutes. Mix together cream and flour until smooth, then pour slowly into soup, stirring constantly. Simmer until thick.

Serve with parsley and cheese on top.

Spicy Hoppin' John Soup

16 SERVINGS

1 pound dried black-eyed peas
8 cups water
16-ounce can diced tomatoes with liquid
8-ounce ham hock
1 cup onion, chopped
1 cup celery, chopped
1 tablespoon salt
2 teaspoons chili powder
1/4 teaspoon dried crushed basil leaves
1 bay leaf
1 cup rice, uncooked

Bring the black-eyed peas and water to a boil; cover, reduce heat and simmer 3 minutes. Remove from heat and let peas stand for 1 hour. Do not drain.

Add tomatoes and liquid. Add ham hock, onion, celery and seasonings. Cover and simmer 1 to 1 1/2 hours until peas are tender. Remove ham hock and debone. Dice meat and return to peas. Add rice; cover and simmer 20 minutes or until rice is tender.

Remove bay leaf and serve.

Spicy Hoppin' John Soup

Coastal Georgia Clam Chowder

12 SERVINGS

1 stick margarine
1 onion, chopped
Three 10.5-ounce cans New England clam chowder soup
Five 10.5-ounce cans cream of potato soup
Two to four 6.5-ounce cans minced clams
2 quarts half-and-half

Sauté onions in margarine. Add other ingredients to onion mixture and place in a large stock pot; bring to a boil, stirring constantly. Reduce heat to low and simmer for 30 minutes.

Beef & Cabbage Soup

6-8 SERVINGS

1 pound. ground beef or bison
1/2 head cabbage, chopped
1 onion, peeled and chopped
3 stalks celery, chopped
28-ounce can diced tomatoes
4 cups water
3 beef bouillon cubes
Leftover green beans, purple hull peas, limas, corn or carrots
Salt and pepper
Worcestershire sauce

Place beef in a large skillet and brown on medium high. Remove beef and drain well.

Place beef, cabbage, onions, celery, tomatoes and water in a large pot and bring to a boil. Add beef bouillon, salt and pepper and remaining ingredients; reduce heat to low. Simmer for 1 to 2 hours.

Easy French Onion Soup

8 SERVINGS

4 onions, peeled and sliced
3 tablespoons butter
6 cups water
6 beef bouillon cubes
1 1/4 teaspoon Worcestershire sauce
1/2 teaspoon salt
1/8 teaspoon pepper
Leftover French bread, toast or roll
Mozzarella cheese, shredded

In a large saucepan, brown onions slowly in butter. Add water, bouillon cubes, Worcestershire sauce and seasonings; simmer for 30 to 45 minutes.

Pour soup into four oven-proof bowls that have been placed on a cookie sheet. Top each bowl with a round of toasted bread and cheese. Slide into oven and broil just until cheese melts.

Whistle Stop Vegetable Soup

16 SERVINGS

2 to 3 pounds beef chuck roast, bone in
8 to 10 cups water
Salt and pepper
1 soup bone
2 medium carrots, sliced
2 cups cabbage, chopped
2 ribs celery, sliced
1 large onion, thinly sliced
1 large potato, chopped
32-ounce can chopped tomatoes, undrained
16-ounce can whole kernel corn
1 cup green beans, seasoned and cooked
2 cups tomato juice
1 cup frozen okra, thawed

Combine the chuck roast, water, salt, pepper and soup bone in a medium-size stockpot; cook until the meat is fork tender. Remove the meat and cut into 1 1/2- to 2-inch cubes; discard the beef bone and set meat aside.

Add the carrots to the beef stock and cook for 20 minutes. Add the cabbage, celery, onion, potato, tomatoes, corn, green beans and tomato juice. Boil until all of the vegetables are tender. Add the okra and cook for 10 more minutes. Adjust the seasonings and add the meat back to the soup.

Serve hot with corn bread.

Whistle Stop Vegetable Soup

Crowd-Pleasing White Chili

12 SERVINGS

Two to three 15-ounce cans white northern beans
6 chicken breasts, cooked and shredded or chopped
Reserved broth from chicken
2 onions, chopped
4 cloves garlic
Chili powder to taste or one package chili seasoning
One to two 10.5-ounce cans cream of mushroom soup
Salsa and sour cream for garnish (optional)

Put all ingredients in crock pot and cook on low as long as desired. When serving, top with salsa and sour cream.

Beer Cheese Soup

6-8 SERVINGS

2 cloves garlic, minced
2 tablespoons butter
4 cups rich chicken broth
1/2 cup all-purpose flour
12-ounce can of beer
1 pound sharp Cheddar cheese, grated
1 teaspoon seasoned salt
1/2 teaspoon black pepper
1/8 teaspoon cayenne pepper

In a heavy saucepan sauté garlic in butter. Reduce heat to medium and add broth; bring to a boil. Whisk flour in beer and add to the saucepan.

Cook until slightly thickened, stirring constantly. Add cheese and seasonings, stirring constantly until cheese has melted.

Salsa Soup

6-8 SERVINGS

TIP

Try South of the Border Corn Bread on page 20.

2 chicken breasts, (about 2 cups, chopped)
4 cups water
Four 15.8-ounce cans of great northern beans, drained & rinsed
16-ounce jar of salsa or picante sauce

Cook chicken breasts in water and drain, reserving two cups of broth. Add beans, salsa or picante sauce and chopped chicken to reserved broth. Bring to a boil, then simmer.

Serve with tortilla chips or corn bread.

Cheesy Chicken Chowder

6 SERVINGS

1 cup carrot, shredded
1/4 cup onion, chopped
4 tablespoons butter
1/4 cup flour
2 cups milk
13-ounce can chicken broth
1 cup chicken, cooked and chopped
2 tablespoons dry white wine
1/2 teaspoon celery seed
1/2 teaspoon Worcestershire sauce
1 cup sharp Cheddar cheese, shredded,

Sauté carrot and onion in butter in a heavy saucepan until tender but not brown. Blend in flour, milk and broth. Stir constantly until thick and bubbly. Add remaining ingredients and stir until thickened. Season to taste.

Fresh Fruit Salad

10-15 SERVINGS

Seedless grapes
Apples, peeled and chopped
Blueberries
Strawberries
Bananas
Fresh or canned pineapple chunks
Kiwi
Mandarin oranges
Sugar or sweetener to taste
21-ounce can peach pie filling

Combine the fresh fruit and sugar in a large mixing bowl. Gently fold in the pie filling. Line a large serving bowl with lettuce leaves and spoon fruit salad over the leaves. Cover and chill until ready to serve.

This is best if prepared the day of serving. Additional fruits of your choice may be added.

Fresh Fruit Salad

Butter Lettuce with Benedictine Dressing

6 SERVINGS

1 small English cucumber
1/2 medium white or yellow onion
1/4 cup parsley, chopped
1/4 cup olive oil
1/2 cup cream cheese, softened
1/2 cup sour cream
1/4 cup mayonnaise
1/4 cup cider vinegar
1/2 teaspoon kosher salt
1/2 teaspoon white pepper
2 heads Bibb lettuce
Salted tomato wedges and toasted pecans for garnish (optional)

Grate the cucumber (skin and all) and the onion by hand or with a food processor. Place the grated vegetables in the center of a clean dish towel, draw up the ends and squeeze out all of the excess moisture. You should be able to extract at least a half cup of liquid and discard.

Make the dressing in a blender by first puréeing the parsley and olive oil until smooth. Add the remaining ingredients, except the lettuce, and blend well.

Arrange cleaned lettuce leaves on a large platter and drizzle with the dressing. The salad may be garnished with salted tomato wedges and toasted pecans if desired.

See picture on page 106.

Mixed Greens with Strawberries & Oranges

6 SERVINGS
MAKES APPROXIMATELY 2 CUPS OF DRESSING

9-ounce package pre-washed spinach
1 head of Romaine lettuce, washed and torn
4 ounces crumbled bleu cheese
11-ounce can mandarin oranges, drained
1 cup strawberries, washed and sliced
1/2 cup toasted pecans

VINAIGRETTE:

1/2 cup balsamic vinegar
3 tablespoons Dijon mustard
3 tablespoons brown sugar
1 large garlic clove, minced
1/2 teaspoon onion, minced
1/4 teaspoon salt
1/4 teaspoon pepper
1 cup olive oil

Toss together spinach, Romaine lettuce, cheese, fruit and nuts in a serving bowl.

Whisk together vinegar and remaining ingredients. Lightly pour dressing over the greens to coat. Place remaining vinaigrette in a separate bowl or store in an airtight container.

See picture on page 106.

Bibb Lettuce Salad with Sugared Pecans

4 SERVINGS

2 tablespoons butter, melted
1/3 cup plus 1 teaspoon brown sugar, divided
2 tablespoons plus 1 tablespoon Kentucky bourbon, divided
2 cups pecan halves
3/4 cup apple cider vinegar
1/2 cup olive oil
2 bunches Bibb lettuce
Crumbled bleu or feta cheese
1/2 cup country ham, cubed

Preheat the oven to 350 degrees. Combine the melted butter, 1/3 cup brown sugar and 2 tablespoons bourbon in a bowl. Add the pecans and coat. Spread the pecans onto an ungreased cookie sheet and bake for about 10 minutes. Let cool.

Whisk the apple cider vinegar, olive oil, 1 tablespoon bourbon and 1 teaspoon brown sugar in a bowl. Place in refrigerator to chill for at least 30 minutes.

Wash and drain the lettuce. Tear the lettuce into bite-size pieces and place in a serving bowl. Add the crumbled cheese and country ham. Toss with dressing mixture and sprinkle with the pecans. Serve immediately.

Bibb Lettuce Salad with Sugared Pecans

Winter Salad

6 SERVINGS

Two parts fresh spinach
One part Romaine lettuce
2 cloves garlic
1/2 cup celery, chopped
1/2 cup grape tomatoes, sliced
1 cup broccoli, chopped
1/4 cup real bacon bits
1/4 cup Sunkist® Almond Accents® or sliced toasted almonds
Your favorite low-fat dressing

Tear spinach and lettuce and place in a large salad bowl. Press garlic and add to the greens along with celery, tomatoes, broccoli and bacon. Top with almonds.

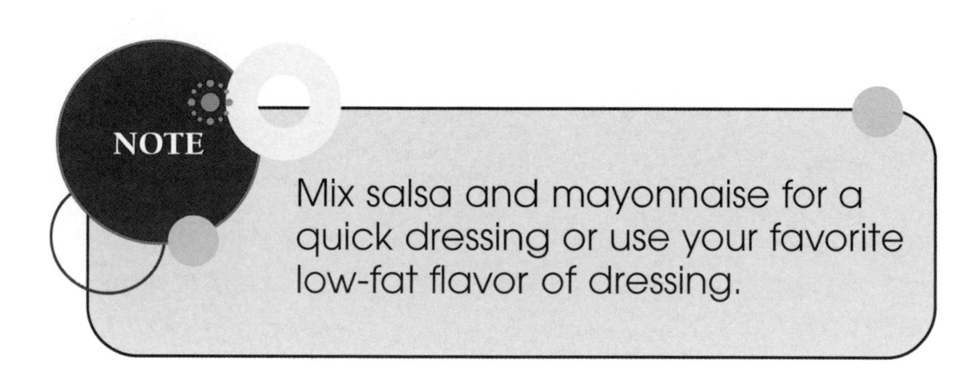

Curried Broccoli Salad

6-8 SERVINGS

2 bunches broccoli
1 cup mayonnaise
1/2 cup sweet pickle relish
1/2 cup jelly or preserves, any flavor
2 teaspoons curry powder
2 1/2 cups red seedless grapes, sliced
1/2 red onion, diced
1/2 cup Sunkist® Almond Accents® or sliced toasted almonds
6 chicken breasts, grilled and sliced (optional)

Cut broccoli into florets and dice, discarding the bottom half of stem. Combine mayonnaise, relish, preserves and curry in a small bowl and whisk. Place broccoli, onion and grapes in a large salad bowl, pour sauce over and mix well.

Chill until ready to serve. Add nuts and mix again before serving. To serve as a main dish, place salad on lettuce leaves and top with grilled, sliced chicken.

Tomato & Mozzarella Salad

6 SERVINGS

2 large tomatoes
1/2 pound fresh mozzarella cheese
Spinach leaves
2 green onions, green part only, sliced
1/8 cup extra-virgin olive oil
Salt
Pepper

Slice the tomatoes and mozzarella. Arrange on a bed of the spinach leaves. Top with the onions and drizzle the oil over all. Sprinkle with the salt and pepper.

Cauliflower Salad

12 SERVINGS

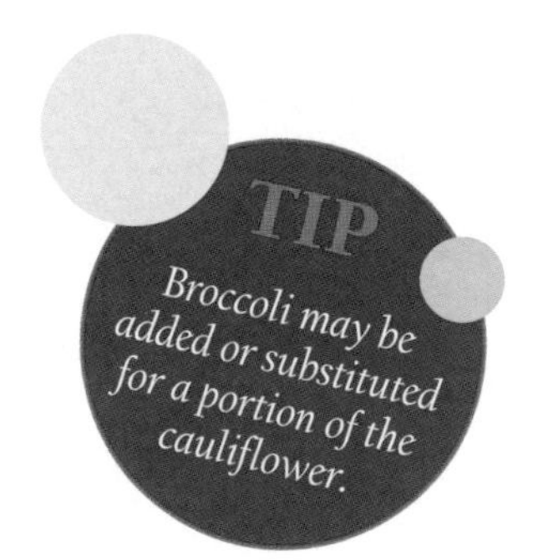

1 head of lettuce, torn into bite-size pieces
1 head of cauliflower, broken in small pieces
2 cups mayonnaise
1 medium onion, chopped
1/3 cup Parmesan cheese
1/3 cup sugar
1 pound bacon, cooked and crumbled

Layer the lettuce and cauliflower on the bottom of a large salad bowl. Combine mayonnaise, onion, cheese and sugar and spread over lettuce mixture. Top with bacon. Cover and chill overnight.

Toss before serving.

Tomato & Mozzarella Salad

Chicken Salad with Wild Rice

12 SERVINGS

10 chicken breasts, cooked and chopped
1 cup celery, finely-chopped
8-ounce can sliced water chestnuts, finely chopped
2 cups slivered almonds, toasted
1 tablespoon lemon juice
1 1/2 cups mayonnaise
6-ounce box wild rice, cooked
1 teaspoon garlic salt
1/2 teaspoon pepper
1/2 teaspoon curry

Combine all of the ingredients and mix. Chill until ready to serve.

Tomato Salad

6 SERVINGS

1/2 cup boiling water
14.5-ounce can stewed tomatoes, with juice drained and reserved
3-ounce package raspberry gelatin
1/2 cup celery, chopped
Bibb lettuce and 3 tablespoons mayonnaise for serving (optional)

Dissolve gelatin in boiling water and add 1/2 cup tomato juice. Stir until completely dissolved, then add remaining juice, tomatoes and celery. Stir well.

Pour into greased molds or a baking dish and refrigerate until set. Unmold or cut into squares and serve on Bibb lettuce leaves. Top squares with 1/2 teaspoon mayonnaise.

See picture on page 107.

Sunflower Coleslaw

12-15 SERVINGS

Two 3-ounce packages Ramen noodle soup, any flavor
16-ounce package slaw mix
12-ounce package broccoli mix
3/4 cup oil
1/2 cup sugar
1/3 cup white vinegar
Salt and pepper to taste
1 bunch green onions, chopped
1 cup sunflower kernels
1 cup slivered almond, toasted

Remove flavor packets from soup mix and set aside. Break apart noodles and place in large bowl. Add broccoli and slaw mix.

Mix together flavor packets, oil, sugar, vinegar and salt and pepper. Pour oil mixture over slaw and broccoli mix and let chill for at least 4 hours.

Take out right before serving and add green onions, sunflower kernels and almonds.

White Asparagus Vinaigrette with Country Ham Crumbles

6 SERVINGS

1 1/2 pounds fresh white asparagus, cleaned and trimmed
1/3 cup red wine vinegar
1 teaspoon prepared yellow mustard
1/2 teaspoon kosher salt
1/2 teaspoon cracked black pepper
1/4 teaspoon dried oregano
1 tablespoon minced shallot
1 cup extra virgin olive oil
1/2 cup country ham, roughly diced in 1/4-inch cubes

Brush the asparagus spears with a bit of olive oil, sprinkle with a pinch of salt and place on a hot grill for 1 or 2 minutes on each side. Remove and set aside.

Whisk together the vinegar, mustard, salt, pepper, oregano and shallot until incorporated and then slowly drizzle in all but a tablespoon of the olive oil in a thin stream, continually whisking until the mixture has emulsified.

Heat the reserved tablespoon of olive oil in a heavy skillet over medium heat and fry the country ham until brown and crispy. Remove the pieces and drain on a paper towel.

To assemble the dish, place the asparagus on a platter, drizzle the vinaigrette over the grilled asparagus and sprinkle with the crumbles. May be served warm or cold.

White Asparagus Vinaigrette with
Country Ham Crumbles

Red Potato Salad with Bleu Cheese & Shrimp

4 SERVINGS

5 cups red potatoes, unpeeled
1/4 cup mayonnaise
1/3 cup Marzetti® Chunky Bleu Cheese Dressing
1/2 teaspoon salt
1/4 teaspoon pepper
3 green onions, whites and some green
1 cup celery, chopped
1 boiled egg
8 to 12 ounces shrimp, thawed, peeled and cooked
Dill weed
1 cup pecan halves, toasted
Spinach leaves
8 asparagus tips, uncooked

Scrub potatoes, chop into cubes and place in a steamer over high heat until tender. Remove and cool.

Combine mayonnaise and bleu cheese dressing in a mixing bowl. Add seasoning, onions, celery and chopped egg; gently stir. Dust shrimp with dill and fold into mixture. Stir in pecans.

Serve on a bed of spinach leaves and top with chopped asparagus tips.

Pasta Salad

6 SERVINGS

8-ounce bag spiral pasta
12-ounce package broccoli and cauliflower florets
12-ounce jar artichoke hearts, drained and rinsed
10 green onions, sliced
1 cup cherry tomatoes, halved
1 cup celery, chopped
2 cups torn Romaine lettuce
1 teaspoon salt
1 teaspoon pepper
1 tablespoon parsley
1 tablespoon oregano
3/4 cup light ranch salad dressing
1/4 cup mild picante sauce
Lettuce leaves (optional)

Cook pasta according to package directions and drain.

Place broccoli and cauliflower into a large mixing bowl. Add artichokes, onions, tomatoes and celery with other vegetables. Gently combine the lettuce with other vegetables. Season with salt, pepper, parsley and oregano.

In a small mixing bowl combine the salad dressing and picante sauce and stir well. Pour over the salad and lightly mix. Cover and chill until ready to serve.

May be served individually or on ruffled lettuce leaves.

Shrimp, Artichoke & Wild Rice Salad

12 SERVINGS

16-ounce box long grain wild rice
1 pound large shrimp in shells, uncooked
12-ounce jar artichokes, drained
1/4 cup olives, sliced
1/2 cup green pepper, chopped
2 green onions, chopped
2 stalks celery, chopped
1/2 cup mayonnaise
1 teaspoon curry
1/8 cup sweet Vidalia onion dressing, or liquid from the artichoke jar
Salt and pepper to taste

Cook the rice according to the package directions and allow rice to cool. Cook the shrimp in boiling water until they turn pink. Drain and cool them using cold water and set aside, then peel and devein.

Combine the artichokes, olives, green pepper, onions, celery and rice and gently mix. Add the mayonnaise, curry and dressing and mix using a large spoon. Add the shrimp, which may be cut into pieces, depending on the size. Mix well, cover and chill until ready to serve.

Shrimp, Artichoke & Wild Rice Salad

Cranberry Salad with Grapes & Apples

8 SERVINGS

2 cups raw cranberries, ground
3 cups miniature marshmallows
3/4 cup sugar
2 Granny Smith apples, unpeeled and diced
1 cup seedless red grapes, sliced
1/2 cup toasted pecans, chopped
Pinch of salt
1 cup heavy cream, whipped

Combine cranberries, marshmallows and sugar. Cover and chill overnight.

Add apples, grapes, pecans and salt. Fold together gently with whipped cream, cover and chill.

Entrées

Savory Swiss Bliss

8 SERVINGS

2 pounds eye of round roast
1 tablespoon butter, melted
1 envelope dry onion soup mix
1/2 cup bell pepper, chopped
1-pound can tomatoes, drained, reserving juice
10.5-ounce can cream of mushroom soup
1/4 teaspoon salt
1 tablespoon A-1® sauce
1 tablespoon cornstarch

Line a 9x13-inch casserole with foil. Place eye of round in pan and add butter, onion soup, pepper and tomatoes. In a jar, shake cream of mushroom soup, salt, tomato juice, A-1® sauce and cornstarch. Pour over steak and cover and seal with foil. Bake at 250 degrees for 2 hours.

Beef Roast in Wine

8 SERVINGS

3-to-4 pound sirloin tip, eye of round or chuck roast
1-ounce package au jus gravy mix
1/2 to 3/4 cup sweet red wine, like Lambrusco

Place roast in the crock pot; mix the au jus package with wine and pour over roast. Cook all day, on low setting at least 8 hours.

Serve with wild rice and vegetables.

See picture on page 107.

Taco Lasagna

6 SERVINGS

1 1/2 pounds ground beef
1 cup onion, chopped
1 1/2 cups green pepper, chopped
4.5-ounce can green chilies
2.5-ounce package taco seasoning
2 cups taco sauce
3 cups Colby-Jack cheese
10 flour tortillas

Brown the ground beef. Add the onion, pepper, chilies and taco seasoning. Spread 1/2 cup of the taco sauce in the bottom of a coated 9 x 13-inch casserole dish.

Layer with 5 of the tortillas, folded in half to fit across the dish. Layer with half of the meat mixture, 3/4 cup of the taco sauce, 1 1/2 cups of the cheese; repeat layers with remaining ingredients.

Bake at 375 degrees for 15 to 20 minutes or until the cheese is melted.

Beef Casserole with Poppy Seed Dumplings

8 SERVINGS

2 pounds beef round steak or sirloin
1/3 cup self-rising flour
1 teaspoon paprika
1/4 cup olive oil
15-ounce jar pearl onions
10.5-ounce can cream of chicken soup
1 soup can of water

SAUCE:
10.5-ounce can cream of chicken soup
1 cup sour cream

DUMPLINGS:
2 cups self-rising flour
1/2 teaspoon salt
1 teaspoon poultry seasoning
1 teaspoon celery seeds
1 teaspoon dried onion flakes
1 tablespoon poppy seeds
1/4 cup olive oil
1 cup milk
1/4 cup melted butter

Cut meat into 1-inch cubes and dredge in a mixture of flour and paprika in a large mixing bowl. Brown meat thoroughly in oil over medium-high heat in a skillet. Transfer to a 9x13-inch baking dish and add drained onions. Combine soup and water in the skillet used to brown the meat and bring to a boil. Pour mixture over the meat. Bake at 350 degrees for 45 minutes or until meat is tender.

Remove dish from the oven. Top with about 10 dumplings. Increase oven temperature to 425 degrees; return dish to oven and bake for 20 to 25 minutes until dumplings are golden brown. Serve with casserole sauce.

To make dumplings, mix together flour, salt, and poultry seasoning. Add celery seeds, onion flakes and poppy seeds. Add oil and milk. Stir until just moistened. Drop rounded tablespoonfuls of dough into melted butter.

To make sauce, mix together soup and sour cream in a bowl and microwave until just boiling. Stir well. Pour the sauce into a serving dish to pass around table for guests to ladle over the dumplings.

Beef Casserole with Poppy Seed Dumplings

Bison Meat Loaf

4 SERVINGS

1 pound ground bison
1 egg, beaten
1 envelope dry onion soup mix
2 cups bread crumbs or oatmeal
1/2 cup ketchup
1/4 cup green pepper, chopped
Salt and pepper
1/8 cup red wine vinegar
1/4 cup brown sugar
1/4 cup ketchup

Mix together the first 7 ingredients. Form into loaf and place uncovered in baking dish in 325-degree oven for 35 minutes.

Meanwhile combine red wine vinegar, brown sugar and ketchup. Pour sweet and sour sauce over meat loaf and continue baking for 10 to 15 minutes more.

German-Style Roast

8 SERVINGS

3-pound chuck roast
Three 27-ounce cans sauerkraut, drained and rinsed well
16 ounces brown sugar
28-ounce can chopped tomatoes and juice
2 medium onions, peeled and thinly sliced
2 Granny Smith apples, cored, peeled and thinly sliced
Freshly ground pepper

Place the roast in a slow cooker and layer with sauerkraut, brown sugar, tomatoes, onions and apples. Cover and cook on low all day until the roast falls apart. Serve over rice, noodles or mashed potatoes.

See picture on page 108.

Bourbonnaised Filet Mignon

6 SERVINGS

Six 4-ounce filet mignons
1 cup Kentucky bourbon
1 tablespoon fresh lemon juice
2 tablespoons butter
1/2 teaspoon kosher salt
1 tablespoon light brown sugar
1 tablespoon brown mustard
1/2 cup heavy cream

Pat filets dry and place in a shallow glass dish. Pour the bourbon mixed with the lemon juice over the dry filets. Cover and refrigerate for at least four hours, turning each filet over to ensure an even marinade.

Remove the filets from the refrigerator and pat dry with paper towels. Season each side with salt and rub with brown sugar.

Melt the butter in a large skillet over medium-high heat. When the butter sizzles, place the meat in the skillet and cook for about 4 minutes on each side. Remove the steaks to a plate: cover to keep warm.

Add the leftover bourbon marinade to a skillet and cook on high. When it begins to boil, whisk in the mustard and cream and reduce the sauce by half. Spoon over filets to serve.

Bourbon-Glazed Rib Eye Steaks

2 SERVINGS

1/8 to 1/4 cup Kentucky bourbon
1/8 cup vegetable oil
1 tablespoon packed brown sugar
1 teaspoon Grey Poupon® mustard
1 tablespoon Worcestershire sauce
1 tablespoon soy sauce
1 large clove garlic, minced
2 rib eye steaks or a cut of your choice

Combine the bourbon, oil, sugar, mustard, Worcestershire, soy sauce and garlic and mix well. Place steaks in a plastic-zippered bag and pour marinade over them. Seal and refrigerate at least 4 hours.

When ready to grill, remove the steaks from the bag, pat dry and grill over medium high heat, turning once, until cooked to desired doneness.

Serve over a bed of rice.

A Simple Stew

8 SERVINGS

1 tablespoon olive oil
1 pound lean beef stew meat
1/2 teaspoon garlic salt
1/2 teaspoon seasoning salt
1/2 teaspoon pepper
15-ounce jar small pearl onions, drained
14.5-ounce can beef stock
10.5-ounce can cream of mushroom soup, undiluted
12 ounces farfalle (bow tie) pasta

Heat the oil in a skillet over medium temperature and brown the meat. Season well. Place meat, onions, beef stock and soup into a slow cooker and cover. Cook on low for six hours.

Serve over cooked pasta.

A Simple Stew

Southwest Noodle Casserole

6 SERVINGS

1 pound ground bison
1 cup onions, chopped
Salt, pepper, and garlic salt to taste
1 1/2 cups chunky salsa
2 cups light sour cream
1 1/2 cups Cheddar cheese, shredded and divided
10 ounces flat egg noodles, uncooked
3/4 cup water or tomato juice

Spray frying pan with cooking spray and brown bison and onions; season. Separately combine salsa, sour cream and 1 cup of cheese. In a sprayed 9 x 12 inch oven-proof dish. Place half the noodles, uncooked, then top with half the meat and onion mixture.

Pour half the salsa/cream mixture over meat. Place remaining noodles on top. Add the rest of the meat mixture and top with sauce. Sprinkle remaining 1/2 cup cheese over top. Drizzle 3/4 cup water or tomato juice over all.

Cover with foil and bake at 300 degrees for 45 minutes, uncover and bake another 15 minutes or until brown on top.

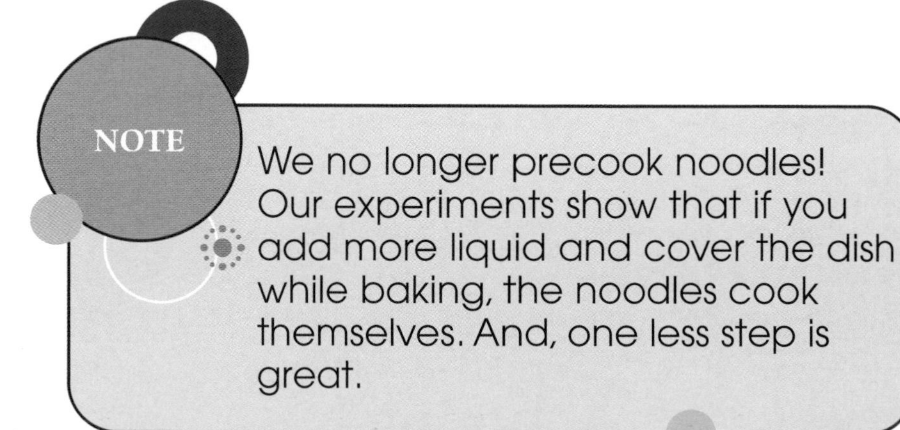

Beef Cabbage Casserole

6 SERVINGS

3-pound head of cabbage
1 cup uncooked rice
1 pound ground beef, browned
1 teaspoon salt
1/2 teaspoon pepper
1 small onion, grated
16 ounces tomato sauce

Cut the cabbage into 8 wedges, removing the core. Cook in boiling water for 6 minutes; drain.

Cook the rice according to package directions. Combine the rice, beef, salt, pepper and onion in a large bowl.

Place half of the cabbage on the bottom of a 3-quart baking dish, then top with half of the meat mixture, repeat. Pour tomato sauce over all and bake at 350 degrees for 1 hour. As it cooks, add water if needed to keep from sticking.

The old recipe for stuffed cabbage called for drained, rinsed sauerkraut on the bottom of the baking dish and top to cover the cabbage rolls. I believe the kraut may be a nice addition for this new recipe.

Barbecued Spareribs

4-6 SERVINGS

3 pounds pork spareribs
1/2 cup onion, chopped
2 cloves garlic, pressed
1 1/2 cups ketchup
1 cup brown sugar
2 tablespoons red wine vinegar
1/4 cup Worcestershire sauce
1 tablespoon prepared mustard
1/2 teaspoon salt
1/2 teaspoon pepper

Divide ribs into 3 racks; wrap each in foil and bake in a 350-degree oven for about 1 hour. Remove and drain liquid. At this point the ribs may be refrigerated until the next day.

Combine remaining ingredients in a saucepan and cook over medium heat for 10 minutes, until onion is translucent. Grill ribs over medium hot coals (about 350 degrees), basting with sauce and turning, for about 30 to 45 minutes.

Garlic Stuffed Pork Loin with Apple Bourbon Glaze

4 SERVINGS

2 cloves garlic
2-pound boneless pork loin
1/4 teaspoon salt
1/2 teaspoon garlic salt
1/4 teaspoon pepper
3 tablespoons olive oil
1/2 teaspoon rosemary
1/2 teaspoon thyme
2 Gala apples, peeled, cored and chopped
2 tablespoons butter
1 tablespoon honey
1 tablespoon Kentucky bourbon

Peel and thinly slice garlic cloves. Cut slits into top of loin, fat side up, with a sharp knife and punch garlic into slits.

Mix together the salts, pepper, olive oil, rosemary and thyme in a small mixing bowl. Place pork loin in an 8x8-inch lightly greased baking dish and rub mixture over the loin, using your hands.

Bake uncovered at 350 degrees for 1 to 1 1/2 hours or until meat thermometer reaches 160 degrees.

Sauté the apples and butter in a large skillet over medium-high heat. Add honey and bourbon and continue cooking over low heat until sauce thickens and apples are soft.

Serve apples over sliced pork.

Baked Ham with Bourbon Glaze

12 SERVINGS

1/2 fully cooked ham with bone in, about 5 pounds
1 cup orange marmalade
1/2 cup molasses
1/2 cup Kentucky bourbon
2 tablespoons Dijon mustard
1/4 cup orange juice

Place the ham in a shallow baking dish and cook, uncovered, at 325 degrees for about 1 1/2 hours.

Combine the marmalade, molasses, bourbon, mustard and orange juice and mix well. Brush the glaze over the ham several times during the baking and cook until the internal temperature reaches 140 degrees on a meat thermometer.

Let stand about 15 minutes before carving. Serve with any remaining glaze.

Baked Ham with Bourbon Glaze

Tuna with Thai Marinade

4 SERVINGS

1/2 cup sesame oil
1 cup soy sauce
1/2 cup fresh lime juice
1/4 cup sherry or sake
2 tablespoons garlic, freshly-minced
2 tablespoons ginger, freshly-minced or grated
1 to 3 tablespoons crushed red pepper flakes (to your taste)
4 thick fresh tuna steaks, about 6 ounces each
Toasted sesame seeds

Combine all the ingredients except the tuna and sesame seeds; stir well. Place the steaks in a glass baking dish and pour the marinade over. Marinate, at room temperature, for 30 minutes, turning the steaks once halfway through. Grill to your preferred degree of doneness. Sprinkle sesame seeds over tuna just before serving.

NOTE

Toast sesame seeds in a skillet over low heat, stirring constantly or on a baking sheet in the oven. Watch carefully as they will toast quickly.

Seafood Wild Rice Casserole

6 SERVINGS

6-ounce package wild rice
1/3 cup onion, minced
1 cup green pepper, chopped
1 cup celery, chopped
2 cups fresh mushrooms, sliced
1 pound fresh or frozen crab meat
1 pound shrimp, cooked and peeled
Three 10.5-ounce cans cream of mushroom soup

Cook the rice according to directions. Add the onion, pepper, celery and mushrooms; mix well. Add the crab meat, shrimp and soup and mix well.

Pour the mixture into a lightly coated 4-quart baking dish. Bake uncovered at 325 degrees for 1 hour.

Creamy Shrimp & Rice Casserole

4-6 SERVINGS

3 cups small shrimp, cooked and peeled
2 cups rice, cooked
1 small onion, diced
1 cup celery, diced
4 hard-boiled eggs, peeled and chopped
Two 10-ounce cans cream of shrimp soup
3/4 cup mayonnaise
1 teaspoon fresh lemon juice
1/2 cup water
3-ounce package sliced almonds
2 tablespoons butter, melted
1 cup dry bread crumbs

Combine the shrimp, rice, onion, celery, eggs, soup, mayonnaise, lemon juice and water in a large bowl. Mix well and spread into a 9x13-inch baking dish.

Mix the melted butter, almonds and bread crumbs and pour over casserole. Bake at 350 degrees for 30 minutes, until hot and bubbly.

Shrimp Samuels

6 SERVINGS

3 sticks butter
1/4 pound brown sugar
2 tablespoons fresh thyme
1 tablespoon fresh rosemary
1/2 teaspoon Tabasco® sauce
1 tablespoon Worcestershire sauce
1 tablespoon minced garlic
24 large shrimp, peeled
1 tablespoon fresh lemon juice
Salt and pepper to taste
1/4 teaspoon cayenne pepper
4 ounces Maker's Mark® bourbon

Melt the butter in a large skillet. Add the brown sugar, thyme, rosemary, Tabasco® sauce, Worcestershire sauce and garlic, Sauté for 2 minutes.

Add the shrimp and cook for about 3 minutes or until pink. Add the remaining ingredients and flame, if desired. Simmer for 2 minutes.

See picture on page 108.

Shrimp & Spinach over Pasta

4 SERVINGS

8 or 9 ounces farfalle (bow tie) pasta
1/2 cup butter
4 green onions, white part only, sliced
5 large mushrooms, sliced
2 cups Parmesan cheese, grated
1 cup nonfat half-and-half or heavy cream, warmed
1/4 cup dry white wine
1 1/2 pounds shrimp, cooked, peeled and deveined
1 cup chopped fresh spinach

Cook the pasta according to the package directions. Drain and keep warm. Melt the butter in a large skillet and sauté the onions and mushrooms over medium-high heat. Add the cheese and stir well. Cook over medium heat for about 2 minutes.

Add the half-and-half and continue stirring until blended. Add the wine and reduce the heat. Add the shrimp and cook over low heat until pink, about 5 minutes, stirring. Add the spinach and cook just until it wilts.

Serve the shrimp and spinach over the pasta.

Shrimp & Spinach over Pasta

Grilled Salmon

4 SERVINGS

Juice of 1/2 lemon
1 clove garlic, pressed
1/4 cup olive oil
1 teaspoon dill weed
1/2 teaspoon salt
1/2 teaspoon pepper
4 salmon fillets

Combine the lemon juice, garlic, olive oil, dill weed, salt and pepper in a small bowl and mix well. Place fillets on a large piece of foil. Pour the mixture on the fish and rub thoroughly with your hands.

Wrap foil tightly to seal package and place on a grill with medium hot coals (350 - 400 degrees). Close lid and cook for about 10 minutes. Be careful not to overcook, as fish dries out quickly.

Citrus Salmon

2 SERVINGS

1/4 cup orange or lime juice
3 tablespoons vodka
0.7-ounce envelope Italian salad dressing mix
1/2 cup olive oil
1 pound salmon fillets

Combine the juice, vodka, dressing mix and olive oil in a blender and mix. Pour into a shallow dish. Place fillets in the dish, turning to coat. Cover with plastic wrap and marinate for 2 hours or more.

When ready to grill fish, discard marinade and grill fish over medium heat for about 12 minutes, or until fish flakes easily.

Grilled Salmon with Cucumber Sauce

4 SERVINGS
MAKES 1 1/2 CUPS OF SAUCE

TIP

If you don't have a grilling basket, place fillets on a grill top which has been covered with lightly oiled foil and punctured with small holes for draining.

CUCUMBER SAUCE
1 medium cucumber
1/2 cup sour cream
1/4 cup mayonnaise
1 tablespoon snipped parsley
2 teaspoons onion, grated
2 teaspoons vinegar
1/4 teaspoon salt
Dash of pepper

SALMON & MARINADE
1 tablespoon butter
3 tablespoons olive oil
2 tablespoons dill pickle juice
1/2 lime or lemon, squeezed
1 tablespoon garlic powder
Black pepper to taste
Salmon fillets

Halve unpeeled cucumber lengthwise and seed. Shred in food processor to make 1 cup. Do not drain. Mix cucumber with the remaining ingredients for the sauce and chill.

In a microwave-proof bowl, mix butter, oil, pickle juice and juice from 1/2 lime or lemon. Microwave mixture just until butter melts. Remove and add garlic powder and pepper, stir. Brush salmon fillets with mixture on both sides and place fillets in grilling basket.

Grill on medium low until fish flakes easily. Serve with sauce.

Grilled Salmon with Pineapple Salsa

4 SERVINGS

1 cup fresh pineapple, chopped
2 tablespoons red onion, finely-chopped
2 tablespoons cilantro, chopped
1 tablespoon rice vinegar
1/8 teaspoon ground red pepper
Four 6-ounce salmon fillets, about 1/2 inch thick
1/2 teaspoon salt

To prepare salsa, combine the pineapple, onion, cilantro, vinegar and red pepper in a bowl and set aside.

Sprinkle the fish with salt.

Heat grill pan or outdoor grill. Cook fish 4 minutes per side or until it flakes easily with a fork.

Top with the salsa to serve.

Baked Chicken with Spinach

4 SERVINGS

9-ounce bag of pre-washed spinach
4 boneless, skinless chicken breasts
2 Roma tomatoes, sliced
1 cup mushrooms, sliced
1 small package dry Italian dressing mix
Balsamic vinegar
1 cup mozzarella or Parmesan cheese, shredded
Angel hair pasta, cooked

Place the whole bag of spinach in the bottom of a 9x13-inch pan. Place the uncooked chicken breasts on top of the spinach. Next put the tomatoes and mushrooms over the chicken and spinach. Mix the packet of Italian seasoning dressing by the package directions but substitute balsamic vinegar for the regular vinegar. Pour the dressing over the mixture and top with cheese.

Bake at 350 degrees for 30 minutes. The spinach will cook down.

Serve over cooked angel hair pasta or rice.

Grilled Chicken & Vegetables

4-6 SERVINGS

MARINADE:
5 cloves garlic, minced
1 cup fresh lemon juice, from about 5 lemons
2 cups extra-virgin olive oil
2 teaspoons smoked salt or kosher salt
2 teaspoons black pepper, freshly ground
1/2 teaspoon red pepper flakes
1/2 cup flat-leaf parsley, chopped
GRILL:
3 boneless, skinless chicken breasts
4 boneless, skinless chicken thighs
2 ears corn, husked and cut into thirds
1/2 pound fresh mushrooms
1 red bell pepper, halved and cored
1 yellow bell pepper, halved and cored
1 orange bell pepper, halved and cored

Combine the marinade ingredients in a medium bowl. Pour 1/2 mixture into a large bowl and combine with chicken breasts and thighs. Toss well, cover and place in the refrigerator to marinate for about 1 hour. Preheat charcoal grill.

Brush the corn with reserved unused marinade and wrap in foil. Toss the mushrooms with 1/4 cup of the reserved unused marinade.

Grill the chicken breasts and thighs to an internal temperature of 165 degrees, about 7 minutes each side.

Grill the corn inside the foil for about 5 minutes each side. Brush the grilled peppers with the last of the reserved unused marinade. Grill the peppers for about 5 minutes on each side. Grill the mushrooms about 2 minutes each side.

Slice the peppers and mushrooms before serving, if desired.

Grilled Chicken & Vegetables

Chicken with Walnuts

4 SERVINGS

1 1/2 pounds boneless chicken breasts
3 tablespoons soy sauce
2 teaspoons cornstarch or flour
2 tablespoons dry sherry
1 teaspoon Splenda®
1 teaspoon fresh ginger root, grated
1/2 teaspoon salt
2 tablespoons vegetable oil
2 medium-size green peppers or 1 red and 1 green
4 green onions, sliced into 1-inch length
1/2 cup walnut halves

Cut the chicken into bite-size pieces and set aside. Blend the soy sauce and cornstarch, stir in the sherry, sweetener, ginger root and salt; set aside.

Pour oil into a large frying pan or wok and heat. Add the peppers and onions; stir fry 2 minutes or until golden brown; remove. Add more oil if necessary and stir fry 1/2 of the chicken pieces. Remove and cook remaining chicken.

Return all chicken to the pan, stir in the soy sauce mixture and cook, stirring until bubbly. Stir in the vegetables and walnuts; cook covered for 1 minute.

Serve over hot rice.

Chicken & Wild Rice Casserole

12 SERVINGS

4 pound chicken breasts, skinned and boned
Two 6-ounce boxes long grain & wild rice
3 to 4 onions, chopped
2 sticks of margarine
3 tablespoons flour
Two 10.5-ounce cans of cream of mushroom soup
1 cup skim milk
15-ounce can sliced mushrooms, drained
Salt and pepper to taste
1 pound sharp Cheddar cheese, grated
Sliced almonds (optional)

Cook the chicken in a large stock pot, cool and chop. Cook the rice according to package directions.

Sauté the onions in margarine; add flour and mix well. Add soup, milk, mushrooms and seasonings to the onion mixture and stir.

Combine chicken, rice and onion mixture in a large bowl and stir. Add cheese and mix; pour into a greased 11x16-baking dish (or two smaller dishes). Top with almonds if desired. Bake at 325 degrees for 20 to 30 minutes.

Poppy Seed Chicken Casserole

6 SERVINGS

1 whole rotisserie chicken
Two 10.5-ounce cans cream of chicken soup
8 ounces sour cream
1 teaspoon poppy seeds
2 cups cooked noodles of your choice
1 cup Cheddar cheese, grated

Remove the meat from the rotisserie chicken.

Combine the soup and the sour cream in a large bowl and stir. Stir the chicken and poppy seeds into the soup mixture and gently fold in the cooked noodles and cheese.

Spray a 9 x 13-inch baking dish. Pour the mixture into the prepared dish and bake at 350 degrees for about 45 minutes or until hot and bubbly.

See picture on page 109.

Cream Cheese & Spinach-Stuffed Chicken Rolls

6 SERVINGS

6 boneless chicken breasts, cut in half
8-ounce package cream cheese, softened
1/2 cup spinach, chopped, cooked and drained
1 small garlic clove, minced
1/8 teaspoon nutmeg
Salt and pepper to taste
1 large egg, beaten with 1 tablespoon water
1/2 cup unseasoned bread crumbs
3 tablespoons butter, melted

Flatten the chicken between sheets of plastic wrap to a uniform 1/4-inch thickness. In a large bowl, beat the cream cheese, spinach, garlic, nutmeg, salt and pepper until combined. Spoon equal amounts of the mixture across the narrow end of each breast. Roll jellyroll style and secure with toothpicks.

Dip the breast in the egg, and roll in the bread crumbs, shaking off the excess.

Arrange the chicken in one layer in a baking dish, seam side down. Drizzle with the butter. Bake at 375 degrees for 25 to 30 minutes or until golden.

Beer Can Grilled Chicken

4 SERVINGS

2 to 3 tablespoons Jamaican-style jerk seasoning, or your favorite dry rub
3- to 4-pound whole chicken
2 tablespoons olive oil
12-ounce can of beer; soda may be substituted

Wash the chicken and sprinkle the cavity with the seasoning. Rub the outside of the chicken with the olive oil and sprinkle with more of the seasoning.

Pour out half of the beer from the can; leave the remaining beer in the can. Punch a couple more holes in the top of the can and carefully lower the chicken cavity onto the can. Make sure the legs come forward to hold the bird upright.

Light one side of a gas grill. Place the can with the chicken on a drip pan on the unlit side. Close the lid and grill about an hour and 15 minutes on high heat, until the chicken is golden brown and registers 180 degrees on a meat thermometer. Carefully remove the chicken from the grill and serve.

Beer C[illegible]d Chicken

Italian Chicken

2 SERVINGS

2 chicken breast halves, skinned and boned
1 medium onion, peeled and sliced
2 cloves garlic
2 tablespoons olive oil
1/2 green pepper, sliced
2 cups spaghetti sauce
1 to 2 cups part-skim mozzarella cheese, shredded

Brown chicken, onions and garlic in olive oil in a large skillet over medium-high heat. Top with green peppers and sauce; cover and cook on low for 25 to 45 minutes. Sprinkle cheese over chicken to melt a few minutes before serving.

Serve with rice or on pasta.

See picture on cover.

Chicken Wrapped in Bacon

6 SERVINGS

6 boneless chicken breasts
6 slices bacon
4-ounces Italian dressing
8-ounce package sliced Monterey Jack cheese

Wrap chicken in bacon. Place in lightly-greased casserole dish. Pour Italian dressing over chicken. Let marinate for about 2 hours.

Bake at 350 degrees for 30 to 40 minutes. Remove from oven and top each breast with a cheese slice. Return to oven for about 2 or 3 minutes or until cheese is melted.

Turkey Brew Burgers

8 SERVINGS

1 1/2 pounds ground turkey
2 cups seasoned bread crumbs
1 cup beer
1-ounce envelope dry onion soup mix
1 cup sharp Cheddar cheese, shredded
1 egg
1 tablespoon Worcestershire sauce
1 tablespoon steak sauce

Combine the turkey, bread crumbs, beer and onion soup mix in a large bowl and mix well. Stir in the cheese, egg, Worcestershire sauce and steak sauce and mix.

Form the ingredients into 8 large patties and broil or grill.

Fettuccini

4 SERVINGS

12 ounces fettuccini
4 tablespoons margarine or butter
3/4 cup Parmesan cheese, grated
1/2 cup whipping cream

Cook fettuccini in boiling water (a big pot so there's plenty of room to swirl it around).

In a medium-sized saucepan melt butter. Once butter is melted, stir in cheese and cream. Stir constantly until smooth over medium to low heat. Remove from heat, add well-drained noodles and mix.

Cheesy Fried Eggplant Sandwich

4 SERVINGS

1 large eggplant, about 1 1/2 pounds
Salt
1 cup dry bread crumbs
1/4 teaspoon salt
6 ounces mozzarella cheese, sliced
2 eggs, beaten
1/2 cup vegetable oil
16-ounce loaf French bread
Lettuce
1 tomato, sliced

Peel eggplant and cut lengthwise into eight 1/4-inch slices. Sprinkle both sides with salt; allow to sit 30 minutes. Rinse eggplant slices and pat dry.

Combine crumbs and salt. Place slice of cheese between 2 slices of eggplant, trimming cheese to fit. Dip eggplant-cheese sandwich in egg and dredge in crumb mixture.

Fry in hot oil until golden brown, cooking a few slices at a time.

Cut bread into 5- to 6-inch portions to fit length of eggplant. Split in half lengthwise and toast. Place lettuce and tomato on four slices of bread, top with eggplant and complete with remaining slices.

This also may be served as a side dish or quartered and served as an appetizer with pizza sauce.

Fried Green Tomato Sandwiches

2 SERVINGS

2 green tomatoes
Buttermilk
Egg
Cornmeal
Olive oil
French bread or your favorite type
2 slices bacon, fried crisp
Mozzarella or goat cheese
Lettuce
Thousand Island dressing

Select firm, green tomatoes that are just beginning to turn red. Cut into 1/2 inch thick slices and soak in the buttermilk for several hours.

Make an egg wash using the egg and a little buttermilk. Dredge the slices in the wash the and cornmeal.

Fry slices in hot oil on one side, flip and fry the other side until slightly brown. Drain on a paper towel.

Place 2 tomato slices, bacon and cheese on each piece of bread. Broil in the oven until cheese is melted. Top with lettuce and a dollop of dressing. Enjoy open face or top with a second slice of bread.

Bourbon-Buttered Cornish Hens

6 SERVINGS

6 Cornish hens, 1-pound each
Salt and pepper for seasoning
1/2 cup butter, melted and divided
1/4 cup honey
1/2 cup Maker's Mark® bourbon

Remove giblets and rinse hens with cold water. Pat dry and sprinkle each cavity with salt and pepper. Place the hens, breast side up, in a shallow baking pan. Brush with 1/4 cup melted butter; bake at 350 degrees for 1 to 1 1/2 hours.

Combine the remaining 1/4 cup butter, honey and bourbon. Brush glaze over hens every 15 minutes during the cooking process.

Bourbon-Buttered
Cornish Hens

Grilled Veggie Burger

4 SERVINGS

2 eggs, beaten
1/3 cup plain yogurt
2 teaspoons Worcestershire sauce
2 teaspoons curry powder
1/2 teaspoon salt
1/4 teaspoon pepper
1 1/3 cups cooked rice, any flavor
1/2 cup walnuts, finely chopped
1/2 cup carrot, grated
1/2 cup onion, chopped
1/3 cup bread crumbs
4 sesame seed hamburger buns
Honey mustard
Hamburger pickles

Combine eggs, yogurt, Worcestershire sauce, curry powder, salt and pepper in a bowl; mix well. Stir in rice, walnuts, carrots, onions and bread crumbs. Shape into 4 patties.

Spray grill with cooking spray and place patties directly on rack. Grill over medium-high for 10 to 12 minutes, turning after 5 or 6 minutes. Serve on toasted buns with mustard, pickles, or your favorite accompaniment.

Grilled Sausage with Onions & Peppers

2 SERVINGS

1 package Italian sausages (approx. 5 per pkg.) or Polish sausage, bratwurst or newer varieties such as the apple-chicken stuffed sausages
2 tablespoons olive oil
2 large onions, peeled and sliced
1 large green bell pepper, seeded and sliced
1 large red bell pepper, seeded and sliced
Buns or a wrap
Mustard
Ketchup

Cook sausages on an outdoor grill over medium-high heat, turning after 5 minutes.

Pour oil into a large skillet and heat on high. Reduce heat to medium-high and cook onions for several minutes. Reduce heat to medium and add peppers. Continue sautéing until onions are slightly browned. Keep warm until sausages are ready.

Place cooked sausages into bun or wrap, top with condiments and onions and peppers.

See picture on page 109.

Chicken Enchiladas

4-6 SERVINGS

2 cups chicken, cooked and chopped
4.5-ounce can chopped green chilies
7-ounce salsa verde (green chili sauce)
6 to 8 flour tortillas
1 ripe avocado
1 pint heavy cream
1/2 teaspoon salt
1 1/2 teaspoons lemon juice
2 cups Monterey Jack cheese, shredded

Combine the chicken, chilies and green chili sauce. Spoon the chicken mixture into one tortilla at a time; roll up each tortilla and place in a coated glass baking dish, seam side down.

Place the meat of the avocado, cream, salt and lemon juice into a blender; pulse until smooth. Pour over the enchiladas; top with the shredded cheese.

Bake at 350 degrees for 20 minutes or until hot and bubbly.

Chicken Enchiladas

Sausage & Rice Casserole

6 SERVINGS

1 pound bulk pork sausage
1 large green pepper, diced
1 large onion, diced
3 stalks celery, diced
1 cup rice (not instant)
4 1/2 cups water
Two 2-ounce envelopes chicken noodle soup mix
1/2 cup sliced almonds, toasted

Brown the sausage in a large skillet. Drain well and place in a large mixing bowl. Sauté the green pepper, onion and celery in the same skillet.

Bring the rice, water and soup mix to a boil in a large pot. Cover and turn heat to low and simmer about 20 minutes or until rice is done. Mix the rice with the sausage and vegetables.

Pour mixture into a 9x12-inch coated baking dish and top with almonds. Bake uncovered about 30 minutes at 350 degrees.

Cranberry Banana Walnut Bread

Recipe on page 22

Crème Brûlée French Toast

Recipe on page 19

Butter Lettuce with Benedictine Dressing

Recipe on page 42

Mixed Greens with Strawberries & Oranges

Recipe on page 43

Tomato Salad

Recipe on page 50

Beef Roast in Wine

Recipe on page 60

Shrimp Samuels

Recipe on page 79

German-Style Roast

Recipe on page 65

Grilled Sausage with Onions and Peppers

Recipe on page 101

Poppy Seed Chicken Casserole

Recipe on page 90

New Potatoes with Garlic

Recipe on page 126

Crusty Grilled Potatoes

Recipe on page 127

Orange Glazed Carrots

Recipe on page 131

Broccoli Bake

Recipe on page 132

Red Cabbage & Apples

Recipe on page 142

Vermouth Asparagus

Recipe on page 136

Cranberry Pecan Stuffing

Recipe on page 146

Cranberry Apple Chutney for Baked Ham

Recipe on page 143

Kentucky Butter Cake with Bourbon Butter Sauce

Recipe on page 159

Pumpkin Praline Bourbon Cheesecake with Gingersnap Crust

Recipe on page 171

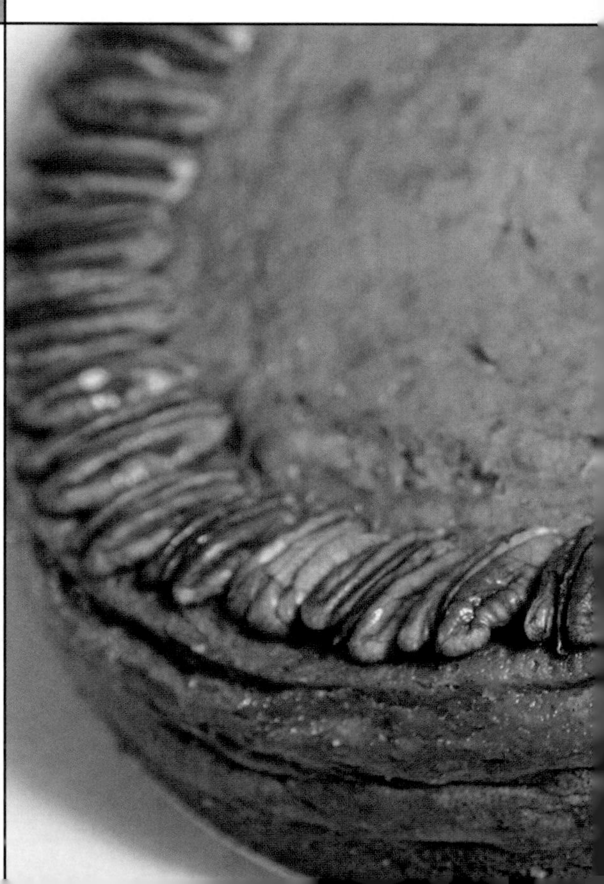

Side Dishes

Bourbon Sweet Potatoes with Pineapple

4-6 SERVINGS

3 cups canned mashed sweet potatoes (also known as yams)
1/2 stick butter, melted
1 cup brown sugar
1/2 cup crushed pineapple, drained
1/8 cup Kentucky bourbon
TOPPING:
3/4 cup granulated sugar
1/2 cup self-rising flour
1/2 stick butter
1/2 cup chopped pecans

Combine the sweet potatoes with the melted butter, add the sugar and pineapple, and mix well. Pour in the bourbon and stir well. Spoon the mixture into a greased, two-quart casserole dish.

Mix together the sugar with self-rising flour. Cut in the butter with a pastry blender until mixture looks like little peas. Add chopped pecans and mix, then sprinkle on top of potatoes. Bake at 350 degrees for 30 to 45 minutes.

Bourbon Sweet Potatoes with Pineapple

Sweet Potatoes & Apples

4-6 SERVINGS

2 large sweet potatoes
4 Fuji apples
1 tablespoon lemon juice
SUGAR MIXTURE:
6 tablespoons butter
1 teaspoon salt
1/2 to 3/4 cup brown sugar
1 teaspoon nutmeg

Peel and thinly slice the potatoes; peel, core and slice apples. Combine the butter, salt, sugar and nutmeg and blend. Place a layer of potatoes in a buttered casserole dish; top with the sugar mixture. Alternate layers of apples and potatoes, ending with the sweet potatoes and topping. Pour lemon juice over all and bake at 375 degrees for 1 hour.

Cheese Grits Casserole

6 SERVINGS

1 cup quick-cooking grits, uncooked
4 cups boiling water
1 teaspoon salt
1 stick margarine
6 ounces garlic cheese spread
2 well-beaten eggs plus milk to equal 1 cup liquid

Bring water to a boil and stir in grits and salt. Return to a boil, then cover and reduce heat. Simmer until mixture thickens slightly. Add margarine, cheese and egg/milk mixture and stir well. Pour into a buttered baking dish. Bake at 350 degrees for 30 minutes and until golden brown on top.

Spinach, Bacon & Potatoes au Gratin

6 SERVINGS

6 russet potatoes, unpeeled and scrubbed
6 slices bacon, diced
1 large onion, chopped
2 large cloves garlic, minced
Two 6-ounce bags pre-washed baby spinach
Salt and pepper
1 cup sour cream
10.5-ounce can cream of mushroom soup
1/2 cup mild Cheddar cheese
1/2 cup Parmesan cheese

Cook whole potatoes in a large pot of salted boiling water until tender when pierced with a fork. Drain, cool and peel.

Cook bacon for 3 minutes on high, add onions, garlic and cook about 2 minutes more. Add spinach and cook only until it begins to wilt. Remove mixture from pan and drain. Season with salt and pepper and combine with soup, sour cream and cheese.

Arrange a layer of thinly sliced potatoes in a greased baking dish, season with salt and pepper, and top with a layer of spinach sauce. Layer again and finish with an attractive potato layer topped with spinach mixture. Bake at 350 degrees for 45 minutes until browned and bubbly.

Creamed Cauliflower Casserole

6 SERVINGS

1 medium head cauliflower
8 tablespoons margarine, divided
1/4 cup flour
2 cups milk
3/4 teaspoon salt
1/8 teaspoon pepper
8-ounce package herb-seasoned stuffing
1 cup water

Break cauliflower into small pieces and cook in small amount of water until tender. Drain and place in a 2-quart casserole dish.

Melt 4 tablespoons margarine in a small saucepan; stir in flour and cook, stirring constantly. Remove from heat and slowly blend in milk and seasonings, then return and bring to a boil, continue stirring. Simmer until thick. Pour over cauliflower.

Combine stuffing, water and 4 tablespoons margarine and mix; spoon over cauliflower and sauce. Bake at 350 degrees for 30 minutes.

Creamed Cauliflower Casserole

Faux Potatoes

4 SERVINGS

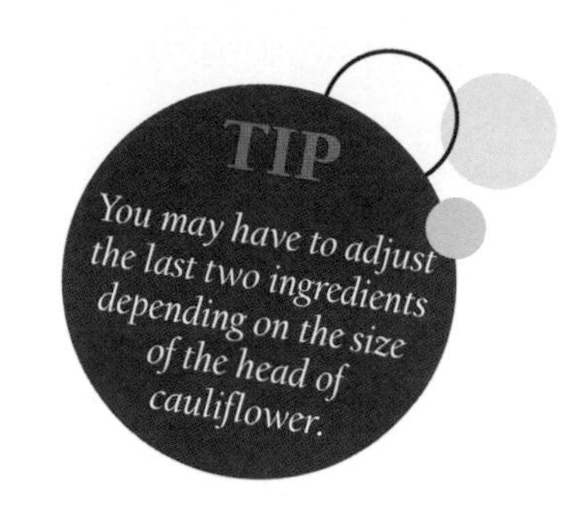

1 head of cauliflower
Salt
Pepper
Butter flakes
1/8 cup Nonfat half-and-half
3 tablespoons Cream cheese

Wash and cut cauliflower into medium-size pieces. Cook until tender in a large steamer; drain well. Place cauliflower in a food processor with seasonings, butter flakes, half-and-half and cream cheese. Purée until the consistency of mashed potatoes. Taste and adjust seasonings, butter, etc.

Hash Brown Potato Bake

6-8 SERVINGS

32 ounces frozen, shredded hash brown potatoes
3/4 cup butter, melted
1/2 cup onion, chopped
10 3/4-ounce can cream of chicken soup
8 ounces sour cream
2 cups Colby cheese, shredded
1 cup buttery cracker rounds, crushed

Defrost potatoes and place in a large bowl. Combine butter, onion, soup, sour cream and cheese and mix well. Pour over potatoes and mix well.

Pour mixture into a 9x12-inch greased baking dish. Sprinkle with crushed crackers. Bake at 350 degrees for about 50 minutes.

Gourmet Potatoes

8 SERVINGS

6 medium potatoes, unpeeled
3 cups Cheddar cheese, shredded
1/4 cup plus 2 tablespoons butter
1 1/2 cups sour cream
1/3 cup green onions, chopped
1 teaspoon salt
1/4 teaspoon pepper
Paprika

Cover the potatoes with water in a large pan and cook until potatoes are soft. Let cool, peel and shred.

Combine the cheese and 1/4 cup butter in a saucepan over low heat. Stir occasionally until almost melted. Remove from the heat and blend in the sour cream, onions, salt and pepper. Fold in the potatoes.

Place in a 2-quart casserole dish and top with the 2 tablespoons butter. Sprinkle with the paprika. Bake, uncovered, at 350 degrees for 40 minutes.

Summer Squash Casserole

6 SERVINGS

1 pound yellow squash, chopped
1 medium onion, chopped
Salt and pepper
Water to cover
1 egg
1 1/2 cups herbed corn bread stuffing mix
1 cup Cheddar cheese, grated
3 tablespoons butter

Place squash, onion, seasonings and water in a large saucepan; cover and bring to a boil. Cook over a medium-high heat until the squash is tender and most of the water has evaporated. Be careful not to burn; lower the heat if necessary.

Remove from the heat, drain and mash. Add the egg, 3/4 of the stuffing mix and 1/2 of the cheese and mix well.

Pour into a greased casserole dish and cover with the remaining stuffing mix and cheese. Dot with a few pats of butter. Bake at 350 degrees for about 30 minutes or until set.

Summer Squash Casserole

Baked Rice

4 SERVINGS

Two 14.5-ounce cans beef broth
1 stick butter, melted
1 cup white or brown rice
7-ounce can sliced mushrooms

Combine all ingredients and bake in a covered casserole dish for 1 hour at 375 degrees. Uncover and bake an additional 15 minutes or until top is golden brown.

New Potatoes with Garlic

4 SERVINGS

12 medium-size new potatoes, scrubbed and halved
1 clove garlic
Water
1/4 stick butter
1/4 cup nonfat half-and-half
1/4 cup real bacon, crumbled
Salt and pepper to taste
Parsley for garnish (optional)

Place the potatoes and a garlic clove in a saucepan. Cover with water. Bring to a boil and cook until tender. Drain well and discard the garlic.

Combine the potatoes, butter, half-and-half and bacon and mix with hand mixer until smooth. Season with the salt and pepper. Garnish with the fresh parsley.

See picture on page 110.

Crusty Grilled Potatoes

4 SERVINGS

1/4 cup olive oil
4 large red potatoes, scrubbed, skin on and cut into nickel-thick slices
1 envelope dry onion soup mix
Garlic salt

Pour oil into a large bowl; add potatoes and toss to coat. Sprinkle soup mix over the potatoes and mix until the potatoes are coated. Place the potatoes on foil sprayed with non-stick cooking spray. Sprinkle with garlic salt. Cover with another sheet of foil and place on top rack of grill. Grill for 30 minutes on high heat.

See picture on page 110.

This recipe can also be baked in a 400-degree oven for about 30 minutes, turning once during baking.

Bourbon Squash Rings

4 SERVINGS

2 large acorn squash, cut into 1/2-inch rings and seeded
4 tablespoons Maker's Mark® bourbon
1/4 cup butter, melted
2 tablespoons brown sugar
1/4 teaspoon nutmeg, freshly grated

Line a baking dish with aluminum foil. Arrange squash rings in a single layer on foil. Prick the squash with a fork and brush rings generously with the bourbon. Let the squash stand for 5 minutes to absorb the liquor. Brush the squash evenly with the melted butter and sprinkle with the brown sugar and nutmeg.

Bake at 375 degrees until tender, about 20 minutes. Serve immediately.

Grilled Yellow Squash

4 SERVINGS

2 large yellow squash
1/2 teaspoon lemon pepper
1/2 teaspoon salt

Wash squash and drain. Cut in half lengthwise. Spray inner side with cooking spray. Sprinkle with lemon pepper and salt. Place face down on top grill rack over medium heat. Cook for about 10 minutes.

Bourbon Squash Rings

Summer Corn Pudding

4 SERVINGS

4 ears of fresh corn
2 eggs
1 cup milk
2 teaspoons sugar
1/4 cup margarine, melted
Salt and pepper to taste

Shuck the ears of corn and cut corn off the cob into a large bowl.

Beat the eggs in a small mixing bowl and add the milk, sugar, margarine and seasonings. Add the corn to the egg mixture and stir well. Pour the corn mixture into a greased 1-quart baking dish.

Bake at 350 degrees for 30 to 45 minutes or until golden brown and the mixture is set.

Orange Glazed Carrots

4 SERVINGS

1 1/2 pounds carrots, cut into 4-inch strips
2 teaspoons flour
1/4 cup brown sugar
1/2 teaspoon salt
1 tablespoon red wine vinegar
1 tablespoon lemon juice
1/2 cup orange juice
1 tablespoon orange peel, grated
2 tablespoons butter

Cook carrots in a small amount of boiling water for 5 minutes. Drain.

Blend together the flour, sugar, salt, vinegar, lemon juice, orange juice and grated peel. Bring ingredients to a boil. Add butter and cook about 5 minutes, stirring constantly.

Pour glaze over carrots and bake, covered, in a 350-degree oven for about an hour. Uncover the last 20 minutes.

See picture on page 111.

This dish may be prepared in a foil-lined pan and frozen before baking. The foil makes the freezing process easier.

Broccoli Casserole

8 SERVINGS

Two 10-ounce packages frozen, chopped broccoli
10 3/4-ounce can condensed cream of mushroom soup
1/2 cup mayonnaise
1 cup Cheddar cheese, shredded
2 eggs
1 small onion, chopped into small pieces
1/2 stick butter
1 sleeve butter crackers, crumbled

Cook the broccoli according to the package directions and drain. Combine the broccoli, soup, mayonnaise, cheese, eggs and onion in a large mixing bowl and mix well. Pour into a greased baking dish. Melt the butter, add the cracker crumbs and mix well. Sprinkle over the top of the casserole. Bake at 350 degrees for about 30 minutes.

Broccoli Bake

8 SERVINGS

Two 10-ounce packages frozen, chopped broccoli
6-ounce package chicken flavored stuffing mix
1 large onion, finely chopped
6 eggs, beaten
1/2 cup Parmesan cheese, grated
3/4 cup butter, melted
1 tablespoon garlic salt
1/2 teaspoon thyme

Cook the broccoli according to package directions and drain well. Combine all ingredients in a large mixing bowl and stir. Pour mixture into a lightly greased baking dish. Bake at 350 degrees for 20 minutes.

See picture on page 111.

Broccoli Casserole

Orange Baked Beans

4-6 SERVINGS

32-ounce can baked beans
1/2 cup brown sugar
1/4 cup ketchup
3 tablespoons frozen orange juice concentrate, thawed
1 tablespoon onion, grated
1/2 teaspoon Worcestershire sauce

Stir all ingredients together in a large saucepan. Bring to a boiling point, reduce heat and simmer, uncovered, for 10 minutes.

Coalminer's Beans

8 SERVINGS

1 pound dried pinto beans
8 cups water or chicken broth
1 ham hock or 1 cup chopped salt pork
2 large white onions, chopped
1/2 teaspoon ground pepper

Soak the pintos in warm water for 6-8 hours; drain and transfer to a large soup pot.

Add 8 cups water or broth and bring to a low rolling boil over medium-high heat. Add the pork, onions and pepper. Reduce the heat and simmer, covered, for 2 hours or until the beans are tender.

Correct the seasonings with additional salt and pepper if necessary and enjoy.

Spring Asparagus Quiche

4-5 SERVINGS

1 pound fresh asparagus
4 large mushrooms
1/2 cup onion, chopped
2 tablespoons margarine
6 eggs, beaten
1 cup four-cheese blend, grated or your favorite grated cheese
2 cups half-and-half
Salt and pepper to taste
Pastry for 9-inch pie crust

Wash asparagus and cut off stems about an inch deep. Slice asparagus into pieces about an inch long. Wash and slice mushrooms.

Place onion and mushrooms in a large skillet with margarine and sauté a couple of minutes.

Beat the eggs in a mixing bowl, add cheese, half-and-half and seasonings; mix well. Add asparagus and mushroom mixture and stir. Pour mixture into the pie crust and bake at 350 degrees for 35 minutes or until golden brown on top.

Orange Mint Peas

4-6 SERVINGS

Two 10-ounce packages frozen peas
5 tablespoons fresh orange juice
2 teaspoons lemon juice
2 teaspoons sugar
2 tablespoons fresh crushed mint
2 tablespoons butter
1/2 teaspoon salt
1/4 teaspoon white pepper
Whole mint leaves and fresh slivers of orange peel for garnish (optional)

Cook peas according to package directions; do not overcook. Drain; add orange juice, lemon juice, sugar and mint. Stir to blend. Add butter, salt and pepper. Serve garnished with whole mint leaves and fresh slivers of orange peel.

Vermouth Asparagus

4 SERVINGS

1 to 1 1/2 pounds fresh asparagus
1/2 cup butter
1/4 cup dry vermouth
2 tablespoons lemon juice
2 tablespoons parsley, chopped
3 tablespoons Parmesan cheese
1 teaspoon paprika

Steam asparagus to desired tenderness. Melt the butter in a saucepan and stir in vermouth, lemon juice and parsley. Heat through and pour over cooked asparagus. Sprinkle with Parmesan cheese and paprika.

See picture on page 112.

Orange Mint Peas

Sautéed Mushrooms

4 SERVINGS

1 tablespoon olive oil
3 tablespoons butter
1 pound mushrooms, sliced
3 tablespoons Worcestershire sauce
1 1/2 tablespoons soy sauce
Seasoned salt to taste
Garlic powder to taste
Black pepper to taste
4 to 5 drops Tabasco® sauce

Heat the olive oil and butter in a skillet. Add the mushrooms, Worcestershire sauce, soy sauce, and remaining seasonings. Sauté over low heat for about 20 minutes.

Rice with Carrots

4 SERVINGS

1 cup long grain rice
2 cups water
1 large carrot, peeled and sliced or shredded
Salt and pepper to taste

Place rice and water in saucepan. Top with sliced carrots and seasonings. Cover and cook on high until boiling; reduce heat to low and cook, covered, until holes appear in the rice, about 25 minutes.

Macaroni & Cheese

6 SERVINGS

8 ounces macaroni, uncooked
1 teaspoon butter
1 egg, beaten
1 teaspoon dry mustard
1 teaspoon salt
1 tablespoon hot water
1 cup milk
3 cups sharp Cheddar cheese, grated

Boil the macaroni in a saucepan, in enough water to cover until tender; drain thoroughly. Stir in the butter and egg and mix well. Combine the mustard, salt, hot water and milk and blend into noodle mixture. Add the cheese to the macaroni, reserving enough to sprinkle over the top, and mix.

Pour the macaroni into a coated casserole dish. Sprinkle with the remaining cheese. Bake at 350 degrees for 45 minutes or until the mixture is set and the top is crusty.

Carrots & Zucchini

6 SERVINGS

1/2 cup butter
4 to 5 carrots, julienned
4 zucchini, julienned
Salt
Pepper
2 tablespoons orange marmalade

Melt the butter in a large skillet. Add the carrots and zucchini. Sprinkle with the seasonings and cook on high for about 3 minutes, or until just tender. Add marmalade and stir constantly. Adjust the seasonings and serve.

Cranberry & Apple Bake

6 SERVINGS

2 cups raw cranberries
3 cups apples, peeled and chopped
2 cups brown sugar, divided
1 stick butter, melted
1 cup quick-cooking oatmeal

Stir the cranberries, apples and 1 cup of sugar in a mixing bowl. Melt butter in a medium saucepan; add oatmeal and remaining cup of sugar and mix well.

Pour the apple mixture into a greased baking dish. Top with the oatmeal mixture. Bake at 350 degrees for 1 hour.

Carrots & Zucchini

Red Cabbage & Apples

6-8 SERVINGS

4 tablespoons butter
1/2 head red cabbage, shredded
3 apples, peeled and chopped
1/4 cup red wine vinegar
1 teaspoon salt
1/2 cup brown sugar or Splenda®

Melt the butter in a large saucepan over medium heat. Add the shredded cabbage and apples. Pour in vinegar, salt and brown sugar and stir mixture over high heat for 2 or 3 minutes. Cook over medium heat for 15 minutes, then simmer until the cabbage mixture has cooked down, about 45 minutes.

Add more sweetener if proportions are not correct; it should have a sweet and sour taste.

See picture on page 112.

Cranberry Apple Chutney for Baked Ham

MAKES 1 QUART

TIP

This makes a great accompaniment to your favorite baked ham.

2 large Granny Smith apples, peeled and chopped
1 pear, peeled and chopped
1/2 cup brown sugar
2 tablespoons butter
1/4 cup cider vinegar
1 teaspoon orange zest
1/8 teaspoon ginger
3/4 cup raisins
16-ounce can whole berry cranberry sauce

Combine apples, pear, sugar and butter in a saucepan and cook about 8 minutes, or until tender. Add vinegar, orange zest, ginger, raisins and cranberry sauce and cook on low for about 15 minutes, stirring. Pour into a serving dish.

See picture on page 113.

Scalloped Pineapple

8 SERVINGS

4 cups bread crumbs, fresh French or sourdough chunks
20-ounce can pineapple chunks, drained
3 eggs, beaten
1 1/2 cups brown sugar
1 cup butter, melted

Combine the bread crumbs and pineapple in a 9x13-inch greased baking dish. Combine the eggs, sugar and butter and pour over the pineapple. Bake at 350 degrees for 30 minutes.

Beets with Pineapple

6 SERVINGS

2 tablespoons brown sugar
1 tablespoon cornstarch
1/2 teaspoon salt
14-ounce can pineapple chunks, drained, reserving juice
1 tablespoon lemon juice
1 tablespoon margarine
16-ounce can beets, sliced and drained

Combine the brown sugar, cornstarch and salt in a large saucepan. Stir in the pineapple juice and cook until the mixture thickens and bubbles, stirring constantly. Add the pineapple chunks, lemon juice, margarine, and beets. Cook over a medium heat until thoroughly heated.

Scalloped Pineapple

Cranberry Pecan Stuffing

6 SERVINGS

6 slices bacon
1 cup sliced celery
1/2 cup onion, chopped
8 1/2-ounce package herb-seasoned stuffing mix
1 1/2 cups wild rice, cooked
3/4 cup raw cranberries, chopped
3/4 cup chopped pecans
10.5-ounce can condensed beef broth
1 egg, slightly beaten
4 tablespoons Maker's Mark® bourbon

Cook bacon until crisp in a large skillet. Pour off all but 2 tablespoons of the drippings. Drain and crumble.

Cook celery and onion in the drippings until tender. Combine bacon, celery, onion, stuffing mix, cooked rice, cranberries, pecans, broth and egg. After mixing thoroughly, add bourbon. If stuffing is dry, add more bourbon or water.

Bake in a round casserole dish at 350 degrees for 30 minutes or make into balls using an ice cream scoop; line the dish with balls, baking for 20 minutes.

See picture on page 113.

Desserts

White Chocolate Strawberry Cheesecake

12 SERVINGS

12 whole chocolate graham crackers, crushed
4 tablespoons margarine, melted
Nine 2-ounce squares of almond flavored bark
Three 8-ounce packages cream cheese, softened
1 cup sour cream
4 eggs
1 cup Splenda®
1 teaspoon vanilla extract
1 cup fresh strawberries, sliced

TOPPING:

1 cup fresh strawberries, sliced
1/4 cup Splenda®

Combine the graham cracker crumbs with margarine. Pat into the bottom and 1 1/2 inches up the side of a 9-inch springform pan. Bake at 325 degrees for about 10 minutes and remove from the oven to cool.

Melt the almond bark in a glass bowl in the microwave or over a pan of boiling water, stirring until melted.

Combine the cream cheese and sour cream using an electric mixer or food processor. Add the eggs, one at a time until combined. Add the Splenda®, vanilla extract and melted almond bark and mix. Stir in the sliced strawberries.

Pour the mixture into the graham cracker crust and bake at 300 degrees for 1 hour and 15 minutes. Turn off the oven, open the oven door slightly and leave the cheesecake in for another 30 minutes. The center will be swishy but will firm up after refrigeration. Chill uncovered overnight. Run a knife around the pan and lift off the side of the springform pan when ready to serve.

Combine the strawberries and Splenda®. Arrange on top of cake.

White Chocolate Strawberry Cheesecake

Kentucky Bourbon Cake

12-16 SERVINGS

18.25-ounce package Duncan Hines® yellow cake mix
3.4-ounce package vanilla instant pudding
4 eggs
1/2 cup oil
1/2 cup water
1 cup Kentucky bourbon, divided
1 cup nuts, chopped
1/2 cup butter
1/2 cup sugar

Combine the cake mix, pudding, eggs, oil, water and 1/2 cup bourbon and mix using an electric mixer for 1 minute on medium speed. Fold in the nuts.

Pour mixture into a greased tube pan and bake at 325 degrees for 50 to 55 minutes.

Heat the other 1/2 cup bourbon, butter and sugar in a heavy saucepan until the sugar is dissolved. Pour over cake while still warm.

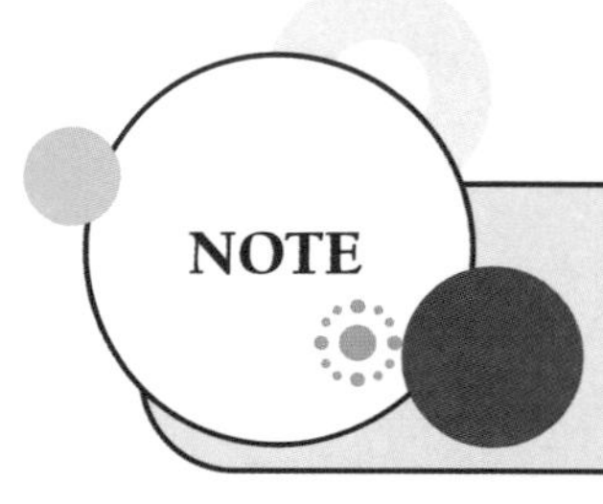

Rum may be substituted for bourbon.

Chocolate Pound Cake

12 SERVINGS

2 1/2 cups all-purpose flour
1/2 teaspoon salt
1/2 teaspoon baking soda
Six 1.55-ounce chocolate candy bars
2 sticks butter
2 cups sugar
4 eggs
1 cup buttermilk
2 teaspoons vanilla extract
1 cup chocolate sauce
Cherries and melted chocolate for garnish (optional)

Sift the flour, salt and baking soda in a bowl. Melt the candy bars and butter in a saucepan. Combine the sugar, eggs, buttermilk, vanilla extract and chocolate sauce and mix well. Add the sugar mixture to the flour mixture and stir. Pour in the chocolate candy bar mixture and stir. Pour the batter into a coated bundt pan.

Bake at 350 degrees for 45 minutes or until done.

Drizzle the top of the cake with extra melted chocolate and garnish with the cherries.

Hot Fudge-Style Cake

12 SERVINGS

1 3/4 cups brown sugar, divided
1 cup all-purpose flour
1/4 cup plus 3 tablespoons unsweetened cocoa, divided
2 teaspoons baking powder
1/2 teaspoon salt
1/2 cup milk
2 tablespoons butter, melted
1/2 teaspoon vanilla extract
1 3/4 cups boiling water

Combine 1 cup of the brown sugar, flour, 3 tablespoons of the cocoa, baking powder and salt in a mixing bowl. Stir in milk, butter and vanilla extract. Spread the mixture over the bottom of a slow cooker. Combine the remaining brown sugar and cocoa in a separate bowl; sprinkle evenly in the slow cooker. Pour in boiling water; do not stir at any point. Cover and cook on high for 2 to 3 hours or until a wooden pick comes out clean.

Fudge Cake

8 SERVINGS

3-ounce package chocolate pudding and pie filling
18.25-ounce box chocolate cake mix
1 cup semi-sweet chocolate chips
1/2 cup nuts, chopped

Cook chocolate pudding and pie filling as directed on package. Blend dry cake mix into hot pudding. Pour into a greased 9x13-inch pan. Sprinkle chocolate chips and nuts on top.

Bake at 350 degrees for 30 to 35 minutes. Serve warm with whipped cream.

Hot Fudge-Style Cake

Brownie Cheesecake

12 SERVINGS

19-ounce package brownie mix
32 ounces cream cheese, softened
1 cup sugar
1 teaspoon vanilla extract
1/2 cup sour cream
3 eggs
Chocolate syrup

Prepare brownie mix according to package directions. Pour into a foil-lined 9 x 13-inch pan. Bake at 325 degrees for 15 minutes until almost done but not quite set.

Beat cream cheese, sugar and vanilla with an electric mixer until blended. Add sour cream and mix well. Add eggs, beating after each addition. Pour mixture over brownie and smooth over.

Bake at 325 degrees for 40 minutes or until center is almost set. Run a knife around edges to loosen and cool.

Refrigerate at least 4 hours or overnight. Drizzle each square with chocolate syrup before serving.

Chocolate Sheet Cake

12-16 SERVINGS

SHEET CAKE:
2 cups sugar
2 cups self-rising flour
1/2 teaspoon salt
1 cup margarine
1 cup water
4 tablespoons unsweetened cocoa
2 eggs
1/2 cup sour cream
1 teaspoon baking soda
ICING:
1 stick margarine
4 tablespoons unsweetened cocoa
6 tablespoons milk
1 pound powdered sugar
1 teaspoon vanilla extract
1 cup pecans, chopped

Combine the sugar, flour and salt in a large mixing bowl. Bring the margarine, water and cocoa to a boil in a saucepan. Pour the hot mixture into the dry ingredients and mix well. Combine the eggs, sour cream and baking soda in a separate bowl. Add to the mixture and beat well.

Pour the batter into a greased and floured 12x17x1-inch cookie sheet pan. Bake at 400 degrees for 20 minutes.

For icing, combine the margarine, cocoa and milk and bring to a boil in a medium saucepan, stirring constantly. Remove from the heat. Add powdered sugar, a little at a time. Add vanilla and mix until smooth. Mix in the chopped pecans; mix well. Pour over the hot cake as it comes from the oven.

Cut and serve the cooled cake with whipped topping or coffee ice cream.

Chocolate-Almond Bavarian

8 SERVINGS
MAKES 3 CUPS OF SAUCE

BAVARIAN:
1 1/2 envelopes unflavored gelatin
2 1/2 cups milk, divided
2/3 cup granulated sugar
1/4 teaspoon salt
1/2 cup slivered almonds, toasted
1 teaspoon pure almond extract
1 cup heavy cream, whipped to stiff peaks
1 1/2 cups chocolate sauce
CHOCOLATE SAUCE:
8 ounces unsweetened baking chocolate
2 cups granulated sugar
12-ounce can evaporated milk
1 teaspoon pure vanilla extract
1/2 stick butter

Sprinkle the gelatin over a 1/2 cup of the milk in a small bowl and let soften.

In a double boiler, combine the remaining milk, sugar and salt. Stir until the mixture is hot and well-blended. Add almonds, stir, remove from the heat, cover and let stand for 15 minutes. Add the gelatin mixture to the almond mixture, set over simmering water and stir until dissolved. Remove from the heat and let cool for 10 minutes, add the almond extract and beat with an electric mixer until fluffy. Fold in the whipped cream, scrape the mixture into a 5-cup ring mold and chill until firm, at least 4 hours. Unmold the Bavarian onto a deep platter, coat the top with chocolate sauce and spoon remaining sauce into the center of the ring.

For chocolate sauce, melt the chocolate over low heat in a large saucepan. Add the sugar and stir until blended. Increase heat to medium; gradually add evaporated milk. Cook, stirring constantly, until the mixture thickens, about 10 minutes. Remove the pan from heat, add vanilla and butter. Stir until the butter melts.

Chocolate-Almond Bavarian

Angel Bavarian Cake

12 SERVINGS

2 cups milk
4 egg yolks
1 cup sugar
2 tablespoons self-rising flour
2 envelopes unflavored gelatin
1/2 cup cold water
1/2 cup orange juice
Rind of 1 large orange, grated
1/2 pint whipping cream
4 egg whites
1 large, store-bought angel food cake
8-ounce container whipped topping
Coconut, toasted (optional)

Combine milk, egg yolks, sugar and flour in a saucepan and cook until thick over medium heat, stirring constantly. Dissolve gelatin in water and pour into hot custard. Cool mixture and add juice and rind.

Separately, whip the cream, then whip the egg whites; gently fold each into the custard. Break cake into small pieces and layer cake, then custard, into a tube pan. Repeat process, ending with custard. Chill overnight.

To unmold, let the cake stand briefly in a few inches of hot water. Invert onto a cake stand.

Cover entire cake with whipped topping. Toasted coconut may be used for garnish.

Warning: Consumption of uncooked egg whites may cause illness.

Kentucky Butter Cake with Bourbon Butter Sauce

12 SERVINGS

BUTTER CAKE:
2 sticks butter
2 cups sugar
4 eggs
1 cup buttermilk
2 teaspoons vanilla extract
3 cups all-purpose flour, sifted
BOURBON BUTTER SAUCE:
1 cup sugar
1/4 cup water
1 stick butter
1 or more teaspoons Kentucky bourbon

Cream the butter and sugar in a large mixing bowl. Add the eggs, beating well after each one. Add the buttermilk and vanilla; stir well. Add flour gradually. Turn mixture into a coated 10-inch tube pan. Bake at 350 degrees for 1 hour. Remove the cake from the oven to cool.

For sauce, combine sugar, water and butter in a saucepan. Heat until butter is melted but not boiling. Remove from heat and add bourbon.

Run a knife along the sides of the pan and prick the top of the cake with a fork. Pour Bourbon Butter Sauce over the cake. Allow to set for 2 hours before serving.

See picture on page 114.

Peach Ice Cream

TIP

This will be soft, so if you want to serve it firmer, pour it into an airtight container and place in the refrigerator for 2 hours.

MAKES 1 1/2 QUARTS

3 peaches, peeled and chopped
1/4 cup sugar
1-ounce package sugar-free instant vanilla pudding mix
5-ounce can evaporated milk
14-ounce can sweetened condensed milk
2 cups half-and-half

Mix the peaches and sugar in a small bowl and let it set at least 30 minutes.

Combine the pudding mix, evaporated milk and sweetened condensed milk in a large bowl, stir with a whisk. Add the half-and-half and mix well. Place mixture in the ice cream machine set to the on position, with the mixing arm in place. Allow to mix about 25 minutes or until it begins to thicken; add the drained peach mixture during the last 5 minutes.

Lemon Ice Cream

MAKES 1 QUART

1 cup whole milk
1 cup sugar
Juice of 2 lemons
Rind (zest) of 1 lemon, finely grated
1 cup whipping cream

Warm the milk in a saucepan over medium low heat, just until it is hot. Do not let it boil or scald. When hot, add the sugar, stirring until dissolved. Remove from heat, let cool, cover and refrigerate until thoroughly chilled.

Stir lemon juice, zest and whipping cream into the milk mixture. Freeze according to the ice cream machine's instructions.

Peach Ice Cream

Lemonade Pie

6 SERVINGS

8-ounce container whipped topping
14-ounce can low-fat sweetened condensed milk
6-ounce can frozen lemonade, thawed
1 prepared graham cracker crust

Combine the whipped topping and sweetened condensed milk using an electric mixer. Add the lemonade in a steady stream while continuing to mix. Pour the mixture into the crust and cover. Chill for 3 hours before serving.

Quick Peach Pie

6 SERVINGS

1 egg
1/3 cup margarine, melted
1/3 cup self-rising flour
1 cup sugar
1 teaspoon vanilla
3 to 4 fresh peaches, peeled and sliced,
  or a 29-ounce can of sliced peaches, drained
Unbaked pie crust

In a large mixing bowl whisk the egg. Add the melted margarine, flour, sugar and vanilla. Mix well.

Place sliced peaches in an unbaked pie shell and cover with egg mixture. Bake at 350 degrees for 30 to 45 minutes or until golden brown.

Peach Treat

6 SERVINGS

1 baked 9-inch pastry pie shell
4 to 5 fresh peaches, peeled and sliced
3/4 cup brown sugar
2 tablespoons all-purpose flour or cornstarch
2 teaspoons almond extract
8-ounce container whipped topping

Bake pastry shell according to directions and allow to cool.

Peel and slice peaches and cover with brown sugar. Allow the peach mixture to sit for two to three hours so that juice will form.

Separate the peaches from the sugared juice. Add flour or cornstarch to just enough peach juice to make a roux. Pour remaining juice into a saucepan, add almond extract and cook on medium high heat; stir in roux. Cook until thickened.

Arrange peach slices in the baked crust. Pour cooled juice mixture over the peaches, cover and chill.

When pie is completely cooled, cover with whipped topping, spreading to the edges. Refrigerate until ready to serve.

Peach Crisp

6 SERVINGS

2 1/2 pounds fresh peaches, peeled and pitted
1 cup all-purpose flour, sifted
1 cup brown sugar
1/4 teaspoon salt
1/2 teaspoon cinnamon
1/2 cup butter, soft

Preheat oven to 375 degrees. Coat an 8-inch square baking dish with cooking spray. Slice peeled, pitted peaches into the dish.

Sift together flour, sugar, salt and cinnamon into a medium-size bowl. Cut butter into the flour mixture with a pastry blender until mixture resembles coarse meal. Sprinkle crumbs evenly over peaches in baking dish.

Bake at 375 degrees for 45 to 50 minutes, until topping is golden brown. Serve peach crisp warm with vanilla ice cream.

Fruit Pizza

8-10 SERVINGS

Two 20-ounce rolls sugar cookie dough
10 ounces vanilla chips
8-ounce package cream cheese, softened
2 cups strawberries, sliced
1 cup blueberries or 1 cup kiwi, sliced

Cut dough into slices and press into a coated pizza pan. Bake at 350 degrees until lightly brown and cool.

Melt the vanilla chips and cream cheese together in the microwave; stir until smooth. Spread the cream cheese mixture over the crust. Arrange the fruit on top immediately before serving.

Peach Crisp

Run for the Roses Pie

8 SERVINGS

1 cup sugar
1/2 cup self-rising flour
1/2 cup butter, melted
2 slightly eggs, beaten
3/4 cup pecans, chopped
6 ounces semi-sweet chocolate chips
1 teaspoon vanilla extract
2 tablespoons Kentucky bourbon
1 unbaked 9-inch pie shell

Combine sugar and flour in a mixing bowl. Mix in butter. Add eggs, nuts, chocolate chips, vanilla and bourbon. Mix well. Pour into pie shell. Place on a baking sheet and bake in a preheated 325-degree oven for 55 minutes until top is golden brown.

Frozen Toffee Cream Pie

6 SERVINGS

Chocolate cookie pie shell
1 cup whipping cream
2/3 cup sweetened condensed milk
1/4 cup strong cooled coffee
1/2 teaspoon vanilla
Two Heath® candy bars, crushed

Whip cream on high speed in a bowl; add sweetened condensed milk, coffee and vanilla. Beat on low speed with a mixer until blended. Stir all but 2 tablespoons of candy into mixture.

Pour mixture into pie crust and sprinkle top with remaining crushed candy. Freeze until firm or overnight.

Derby Time Homemade Ice Cream

MAKES 1 GALLON

1 1/2 cups chopped pecans
3 tablespoons butter, melted
1 gallon whole milk
2 1/2 cups sugar
4 egg yolks, beaten
3/8 cup Kentucky bourbon
2 tablespoons vanilla flavoring
3 tablespoons imitation butter and nut flavoring
12-ounce package semi-sweet chocolate mini morsels

Preheat oven to 400 degrees. Stir butter into chopped pecans and toast. Remove from the oven and set aside.

Whisk 4 cups milk, sugar, beaten egg yolks and bourbon. Bring to a boil. Boil 3 minutes, whisking continuously. Remove from heat and cool. Stir flavorings, pecans and chocolate chips into mixture. Pour into a one-gallon ice cream freezer.

If mixture doesn't fill freezer to its capacity, use the remaining milk to fill and stir. Follow appliance directions.

Cake Mix Chocolate Chip Cookies

MAKES 6 DOZEN

18.25-ounce package yellow cake mix
1/3 cup + 2 tablespoons brewed coffee
1/2 stick butter, melted
1 egg
6 ounces semi-sweet chocolate chips

Combine cake mix and coffee in a large mixing bowl and stir. Add the melted butter and egg; beat with a hand mixer until thoroughly mixed. Stir in chips and mix well. Dough will be stiff.

Spray baking sheets with non-stick cooking spray. Drop cookie dough by tablespoonfuls onto baking sheet and bake in a 350-degree oven for about 12 to 14 minutes. Let cool for 2 minutes, then transfer to cooling rack or foil to cool completely.

Cake Mix Chocolate Chip Cookies

Easy Apple Pie

6-8 SERVINGS

1 egg
1/3 cup margarine, melted
1 cup brown sugar
1/3 cup self-rising flour
1 teaspoon almond extract
3 cups apples, peeled and sliced
1 unbaked deep-dish pie crust

Beat the egg in a mixing bowl with a whisk. Add the melted margarine, sugar and flour, mixing well. Add almond extract and mix. Place apples on the pie crust. Pour the egg mixture over the apples. Bake at 350 degrees for 45 to 60 minutes.

Pumpkin Pie Tarts

12 SERVINGS

2 eggs
15-ounce can pumpkin
14-ounce can sweetened condensed milk
1 teaspoon ground cinnamon
1/2 teaspoon almond extract
One 9-inch pie crust, refrigerated

Beat eggs lightly in a large bowl. Stir in the pumpkin, milk and seasonings. Mix well.

Roll out pie crust on a floured surface and cut circles using a plastic cup or cookie cutter to fit into lightly greased muffin tins. One pastry will fill 12 tins. Pour pumpkin mixture into crusts.

Bake at 350 degrees for about 35 minutes or until knife inserted into center of one tart comes out clean.

Pumpkin Praline Bourbon Cheesecake with Gingersnap Crust

12 SERVINGS

1 cup gingersnap cookies, finely crushed
4 tablespoons butter, melted
2 cups brown sugar
Three 8-ounce packages cream cheese, room temperature
3 eggs
2 tablespoons self-rising flour
2 teaspoons Kentucky bourbon
1/2 cup pumpkin pie filling
1/2 cup chopped pecans
Whipped cream and whole pecans for garnish (optional)

Combine gingersnap cookies and butter and mix well. Pat crumbs into the bottom of a 9-inch springform pan and set aside.

Combine sugar and cream cheese in a food processor or mixer and mix well. Add eggs and flour and mix again. Pour in bourbon, pumpkin pie filling and pecans and pulse until just blended. Pour mixture into the crust.

Bake at 350 degrees for 1 hour or until the cheesecake appears set. Cool completely, cover and refrigerate for at least 8 hours. To serve, remove sides of pan and decorate with whipped cream or whole pecans.

See picture on page 114.

You may mix together 1/2 cup canned pumpkin, 1/8 cup sugar, 1/8 teaspoon nutmeg and 1/4 teaspoon cinnamon if you do not have the canned pumpkin pie filling.

No-Bake Orange Coconut Balls

MAKES 6 DOZEN

1 stick butter or margarine
16-ounce box powdered sugar
6-ounce can orange juice concentrate, thawed
12-ounce box vanilla wafers, finely crushed
7-ounce package sweetened coconut

Cream butter and sugar in a large bowl. Add juice and wafers and mix. Pinch off small amounts and roll into balls the size of a dime. Roll balls in the coconut and place in a covered container. Refrigerate until ready to serve.

Toffee Candy

FILLS AN 8-INCH COOKIE TIN

12-ounce package milk chocolate chips
2 cups sliced almonds, roasted
2 sticks butter
1 cup sugar
3 tablespoons water

Combine half of the chips and half of the almonds in a buttered 9x13-inch pan. Cook the butter, sugar and water to hard crack stage in a heavy saucepan. Pour the sugar mixture over the chips and almonds. Add the remaining half of the chips and almonds and smooth. Let the mixture harden and break into pieces.

No-Bake Orange Coconut Balls

Science Hill Inn Biscuit Pudding with Bourbon Sauce

8 SERVINGS

One 10-count can of 1 1/2-inch refrigerator biscuits
1 quart milk
6 eggs
2 cups sugar
2 tablespoons vanilla
2 tablespoons butter, melted
Bourbon Sauce

BOURBON SAUCE:

1/2 cup butter, melted
1 cup sugar
1 egg, beaten
1/3 cup Kentucky bourbon

Cook biscuits according to the package instructions. Break biscuits into small pieces in large bowl. Add milk; soak for 5 minutes. Beat eggs with sugar and vanilla and add to mixture.

Pour melted butter into 2-quart baking dish, add pudding and bake until set at 350 degrees for about 1 hour. Serve warm with Bourbon Sauce, below.

Melt butter in a heavy saucepan over medium heat. Add sugar and cook 5 minutes, stirring constantly. Beat 1 egg in a bowl. Gradually add butter mixture whisking constantly. Add bourbon and serve.

No Crust Chocolate Pie

6 SERVINGS

2 squares unsweetened Baker's Chocolate®
1 stick of margarine
2 eggs
1 cup sugar
1/4 cup self-rising flour
1 teaspoon vanilla extract
Strawberries for garnish (optional)

Melt the chocolate and margarine over low heat, stirring often. Set aside and allow to cool.

Whisk together eggs and sugar in a large mixing bowl. Pour the chocolate mixture into the egg mixture. Add the flour and vanilla and mix well.

Pour the mixture into a greased pie pan and bake at 350 degrees for 25 or 30 minutes. The center will be a bit soft and the outside crusty. Freezes well.

Add a strawberry for garnish. Serve with ice cream or whipped topping.

NOTE

For a quick substitute for Baker's Chocolate® combine 6 tablespoons cocoa plus 2 tablespoons margarine or shorting.

Great Crunchy Cookies

MAKES 6-8 DOZEN

1 cup butter
1 cup sugar
1 cup brown sugar, firmly packed
1 egg
1 cup vegetable oil
1 1/2 cups regular oats
1 teaspoon vanilla extract
1/2 teaspoon salt
3 1/2 cups self-rising flour
1 cup Grape Nuts®
1 cup coconut
1 cup chopped pecans

Cream butter and sugars together in a food processor or mixer until light and fluffy. Add the egg, oil, oats, vanilla extract and salt and mix well. Add 1/3 of the flour and mix. Continue adding the remaining flour until mixed well. (You may have to transfer it into a larger bowl and mix by hand with a large wooden spoon.) Add the Grape Nuts®, coconut and pecans.

Pinch off the dough and roll into quarter size balls. Place dough balls on an ungreased baking sheet and press down with a fork or with your hands.

Bake at 350 degrees for 10 to 12 minutes or until lightly brown. Cool and store in an airtight container.

Great Crunchy Cookies

Pecan Tassies with Cream Cheese Pastry

12 SERVINGS

PASTRY:
3 ounces cream cheese
1/2 cup butter or margarine, melted
1 cup self-rising flour
FILLING:
2 eggs
2 tablespoons butter, softened
Dash of salt
1 1/2 cups brown sugar
2 teaspoons vanilla extract
1 1/3 cup chopped pecans

Blend cream cheese and butter in a mixing bowl. Add the flour and mix well.

Chill dough at least one hour. Roll into tiny balls and with floured fingers, press the dough across the bottom and up the sides of miniature muffin tins.

Beat eggs with a whisk and add softened butter, salt, brown sugar and vanilla extract. Stir in pecans. Drop by teaspoon full into the unbaked dough crusts.

Bake at 325 degrees 25 to 30 minutes.

Million Dollar Cookies

MAKES 5-6 DOZEN

2 sticks unsalted butter
1 cup brown sugar
1 cup granulated sugar
2 eggs
1 teaspoon vanilla extract
2 1/2 cups old-fashioned oats
2 cups self-rising flour
1 teaspoon baking soda
4-ounce chocolate candy bar
12-ounce package semi-sweet chocolate chips
1 1/2 cups chopped pecans

Cream the butter and sugars in a large mixing bowl. Beat in the eggs and vanilla extract. Grind the oats in a food processor and add to butter and sugar mixture. Add the flour, soda and grated candy bar and mix well. Stir in the chocolate chips and nuts. Drop by the tablespoon full about 2 inches apart on a coated baking sheet.

Bake at 375 degrees for about 10 minutes.

Sugar Cookies for Santa

MAKES 6 DOZEN

COOKIES:
2 sticks unsalted butter
2 cups sugar
2 eggs
1/2 teaspoon vanilla extract
1/2 cup milk
4 1/2 cups self-rising flour
ICING:
4 cups powdered sugar
1 cup shortening
1 1/2 tablespoons milk
Food coloring

Cream butter and sugar together using an electric mixer until fluffy. Add the eggs, vanilla and milk and mix well. Gradually add the flour until all is blended. Cover and chill dough for at least 1 hour.

Divide the dough and work with 1/2 at a time. Roll the dough out on a floured surface and cut out cookies using Christmas cookie cutters. Carefully lift cookies onto a greased baking sheet and bake at 375 degrees for 8 to 10 minutes.

For icing, cream the sugar and shortening well using an electric mixer. Add the milk and mix until smooth. Divide icing into, separate bowls according to the colors you want to make. Add small amounts of food coloring to each bowl and mix well.

Spoon the icing into small plastic storage bags and cut off the corners to make piping bags. Decorate the cooled cookies using icing, sprinkles, raisins, nuts or candies.

Sugar Cookies for Santa

Chocolate Mint Kisses

MAKES 5 DOZEN

2 egg whites
3/4 cup sugar
1/2 teaspoon peppermint extract
Green food coloring
6-ounces semi-sweet chocolate chips

Beat room temperature egg whites with a mixer until stiff, gradually adding the sugar. Add the peppermint extract and food coloring. Stir in the chocolate chips.

Drop the mixture by heaping spoonfuls onto an uncoated baking sheet. Place in 350 degree preheated oven and turn oven off. Allow the kisses to remain in the closed oven for at least 8 hours. Remove and store in an airtight container.

Fabulous Fudge

24 SERVINGS

2/3 cup unsweetened cocoa
3 cups sugar
1/8 teaspoon salt
1 1/2 cups milk
1/2 stick butter
1 teaspoon vanilla extract

Combine the cocoa, sugar, salt and milk in a medium saucepan. Cook over medium heat to hard ball stage (250-266 degrees), then remove from heat. Add the butter and vanilla extract. Beat thoroughly using a wooden spoon. Pour the mixture into a lightly buttered 9x13-inch baking dish. Allow to set at room temperature until firm, about 30 minutes.

Chocolate Bourbon Fudge

MAKES 2 DOZEN

12-ounce package semi-sweet chocolate morsels
14-ounce can sweetened condensed milk
1/4 cup Kentucky bourbon
1/2 cup chopped pecans, divided

Place morsels in a microwave-safe bowl. Add sweetened condensed milk. Cover loosely and microwave on high for 1 minute and 30 seconds. Mix with a spatula. Cover and return to the microwave for another 30 seconds on high. Remove and stir well. Add bourbon and stir again until all ingredients are mixed and chocolate is melted.

Place half of the pecans in a greased 8x8-inch pan. Pour half of the chocolate mixture over the nuts, top with remaining nuts and pour the remaining chocolate mixture into the pan. Cover with plastic and refrigerate until firm.

Tiger Butter

MAKES 24 PIECES

1 pound vanilla almond bark coating
1/2 cup chunky peanut butter
1 cup semi-sweet chocolate morsels

Line a 15 1/2-x10 1/2-inch jellyroll pan with non-stick aluminum foil.

Break the almond bark into 1-inch pieces and place in a 1 1/2-quart microwave-safe bowl. Microwave on high for 1 to 2 minutes or until melted. Stir until smooth.

Add the peanut butter and microwave on high for 2 minutes or until melted. Stir again until smooth. Microwave an additional 30 seconds if needed and spread the mixture into the pan.

Melt the chocolate morsels in a 2-cup microwave-safe measuring cup on high for 1 to 2 minutes. Pour the melted chocolate over the peanut butter mixture and swirl through with a knife.

Cool and break into pieces. Store in an airtight container.

Tiger Butter

Chocolate Brickle

FILLS A 3-QUART CONTAINER

Vegetable cooking spray
12 graham crackers
1 cup butter
1 cup sugar
12-ounce package semi-sweet chocolate morsels
6 ounces almond brickle chips

Line a 15x10x1-inch pan with foil and coat with spray. Place graham crackers in a single layer to cover the pan. Combine butter and sugar in a saucepan and bring to a boil over medium heat, stirring constantly. Boil 1 1/2 to 2 minutes without stirring. Pour mixture over crackers.

Bake at 350 degrees for 8 minutes. Remove from the oven and sprinkle with chocolate chips. Let stand until morsels are soft enough to spread smoothly. Sprinkle with brickle. Cool overnight, then break into pieces. Store in an airtight container.

Index

P

Acknowledgements

Just beginning a list of the people who have helped build *Kentucky Monthly's* cooking section is a daunting task. Where to start? And with any list of "thank-yous," you're certain to leave someone out. Hopefully that's not the case here.

First, *Kentucky Monthly* is grateful to **Paula Cunningham** and **Michelle Stone** and the rest of the "Cookbook Ladies" at McClanahan Publishing, who have helped with cooking in some way or another for most of these first 10 years.

During much of this decade, it's been Louisville-based photographer **Wales Hunter's** images and art director **Kelli Schreiber's** eye for design that have enabled *Kentucky Monthly* to present the prepared dishes in such high fashion. Add **Kendall Shelton's** organizational skills to the mix and we hope we have delivered a collection that is worthy of our efforts.

Among those other folks *Kentucky Monthly* should probably thank are: food writer **David Dominé**; the staff of Sullivan University—including Chancellor **A.R. "Al" Sullivan**, President **Glenn Sullivan**, Chefs **Danielle Demaré** and **Derek Spendlove**, and many of Sullivan's students; Richmond-based photographer **Tim Webb**; copy editors **Madelynn Coldiron** and **Ted Sloan**; food historian **Sheryl Vanderstel**; the crew at Publisher's Press; the rest of the *Kentucky Monthly* staff, past and present; and the board of directors of Vested Interest Publications.

But mostly *Kentucky Monthly* thanks those who enjoy cooking and have added the magazine and now this volume to your kitchen reading materials.

Stephen M. Vest
Editor & Publisher